*Mike Harris
Made Me
Eat My Dog*

Mike Harris Made Me Eat My Dog

LINWOOD BARCLAY

ECW PRESS

CANADIAN CATALOGUING IN PUBLICATION DATA

Barclay, Linwood
Mike Harris made me eat my dog

ISBN 1-55022-368-2

1. Ontario — Politics and government —
1995– – Humor.   1. Title.

PS8553.A7433M54 1998   971.3'04   C98-931408-1
PR9199.3.B37M54 1998

Illustrations by Steve Nease.

Cover photo by Rob Allen.

Imaging by ECW Type & Art, Oakville, Ontario.
Printed by Marc Veilleux Imprimeur, Boucherville, Québec.

Distributed in Canada by General Distribution Services,
30 Lesmill Road, Don Mills, Ontario M3B 2T6.

We are grateful for the support of the Ontario Arts Council,
The Canada Council, and the Department of Canadian Heritage.

Published by ECW PRESS,
2120 Queen Street East, Suite 200,
Toronto, Ontario M4E 1E2.

www.ecw.ca/press

To Mike H. Has anyone done more to get the public concerned about the future of Ontario?

CONTENTS

"Mike Harris made me eat my dog."

PROTEST BUTTON

"These days, anyone can be premier."

SPEAKER CHRIS STOCKWELL,
TORY MPP FOR ETOBICOKE

Would You Let These Guys Finish Off Your Basement?

Here's a test for judging any government. Not just the current occupiers of Queen's Park, but any band of politicians out there. Provincial, municipal, federal, whatever. Ask yourself this: Would you let these guys finish off your basement?

This is the question Angus Reid's pollsters should be asking. Not: "If an election were held today, who would you vote for?" And forget: "Which of the three leaders do you feel is doing the best job?" Instead, how about: "If you had to let one of the three major parties into your home to, say, redo your kitchen, which party would it be?"

People care a great deal about changes made to their house. You can screw up a province all you want, but mess up someone's ceramic tile job and you're going to hear about it.

Let's consider specifically the Progressive Conservative government of Mike Harris, elected with 82 out of 130 seats in Ontario in 1995, turfing out the New Democrats — a nice bunch of guys to be sure, but not the kinds of folks you'd trust even for a job as simple as resurfacing your driveway. We've had more than three years to assess Harris and his highly hyped Common Sense Revolution. So here's the question:

Would you let Mike Harris and his team do your rec room?

And if the answer is no, why are you letting them run an entire province?

We decided to test this theory ourselves. Our basement was unfinished and we wanted the area turned into a cozy family room. A place to watch TV, maybe play a little pool or ping-pong, a hangout where the kids could entertain their friends. We were determined not to hire again Rae Days Construction and Consulting, who built our family room. These guys did way more consulting than construction. Their foreman, a decent guy named Bob and the only Rhodes scholar I ever saw swing a hammer, would ask: "Is it okay if I put this nail here? You okay with our putting up this piece of drywall? Shall I go ahead and caulk this window?"

Yes! Yes! For the love of god, Yes! There were days, you just wanted to take a nail gun and shoot yourself in the head. We swore that if we ever did any more work around the house, we'd hire some take-charge guys who didn't find it necessary to form a committee when screwing on a switch-plate.

So we called Invent-a-Crisis Renovating. And I'll tell you, it was an eye-opener, to be sure. I kept a diary of the construction process:

■ Monday:

"Just call me Mike," said the head guy, getting out of his former radar van and adjusting the utility belt around his waist. He had that sucker weighed down. There was a carpet knife, a utility knife and a Swiss Army knife, in addition to a steel hatchet and a long-handled axe. The other guys in his crew started bringing in the things they would need, including a bowsaw, a gas-powered chainsaw, a hacksaw, an aggressive tooth saw, a bandsaw, two-speed scroll saw, a compound mitre saw, a deluxe bench saw, a reciprocating saw, a heavy-duty orbital jigsaw, a circular saw, and a small package of Band-Aids.

I took Mike downstairs and explained the job. Some warm wood panelling, a wall here, another there, a two-piece bath off in the corner, and a bar arrangement like a lot of homeowners put in their basements. Maybe a spot for a small fridge.

Mike sure *appeared* to be listening. He took notes, nodded. Finally, he said: "I think what we have here is a mandate for change."

"Well, sure," I said. "And some track lighting would look good, too."

■ Tuesday:

They started early. The noise! There was a constant racket coming from downstairs. I wanted to go down and look at one point, but Mike stood in the way of the basement door and told me not to worry.

Late in the day I was upstairs, having a soak in the tub, when Mike strolled into the bathroom and began taking measurements.

"What are you doing?" I asked, moving my rubber ducky to maintain my modesty. Mike said nothing and walked out.

■ Wednesday:

Work started early. We were still in bed when Mike and the crew came into the bedroom and started cutting holes in the floor. My furry slippers dropped right down into the kitchen.

"Hold on a sec!" I said. "We didn't sign on for this!" But Mike had some of those industrial earplugs shoved so far in they were meeting in the middle, and paid no attention to me.

I tried to sit him down in the kitchen, but his crew wouldn't let me get near him, even though I'd heard him make a statement on CNN* that he was prepared to meet with me at any time. I made

---

* Construction News Network.

up a sign that read "Mike: Please Listen to Me!" and paraded out front of the house, but this proved to be a bad move strategically because he locked me out of my own home and barricaded the place.

I called a news crew out to the neighbourhood, to make my case that Mike was moving too far too fast, making changes we'd never agreed to. When reporters cornered Mike for his comments, he mocked me: "Well, of course he'd say that, wouldn't he? It's his house, after all, and he's motivated solely by self interest. But I'm here to tell you, this is one renovator who's not about to cater to vested interests."

When they were coming back from lunch, I attempted to block their path into my house, but I ran into a little trouble with some OPP riot squad officers, decked out in Darth Vader gear, who'd been hired on by Mike to make sure things didn't get out of hand. When I stood in front of Mike, the riot squad officers, who had been trained in the most up-to-date negotiating techniques so as to defuse tense situations peacefully, beat the crap out of me.

I was taken to hospital.

■ Thursday:

Nothing much happened.

■ Friday:

Ditto.

■ Saturday:

I finally got to see an emergency room doctor, but because I didn't have my OHIP card with me (it was in my barricaded house) I was refused treatment. By the time I got back to my place, Mike and the guys were packing up.

My house appeared to have been completely demolished, then rebuilt with scraps. Oddly enough, it was now joined to the houses on either side of it.

"What we decided to do," Mike explained, "was amalgamate your home with those of your neighbours. This will make things much more efficient and reduce duplication. Instead of three kitchens and three furnaces and three bathrooms, there will now be just one of each. Of course, there was some downsizing involved. You hardly need three dads under this new arrangement, so we're letting you go. Here's your hat, what's your hurry. And listen, if you're ever having any more work done in the future, be sure to keep us in mind."

And he got in his van and drove away.

So now I take you back to the original point, which was whether you'd hire the Tories to do your rec room. Given my experience, next time I'd probably go with someone else.

But the Tories would argue that you don't have to know everything to run a province. It's not detailed, exacting work like home improvement. A lot of days, you can just wing it. Mike Harris

himself would tell you that what you really need is a good dose of common sense. His own father, Deane, was once quoted as saying "running the province is no different than running a pro shop," another job you'd find on Mike's cv.

One wonders what a pro shop and golf course, run the same way Mike Harris runs Ontario, would be like. In the interests of efficiency, the par 5s would be cut back to par 4s. The grounds crew would be told that independent test scores found that greens in Alberta were much better tended than those in this province. And if that bit of news didn't improve morale enough, a 4-iron upside the head would have to be employed to ensure that dispositions improved.

We're now more than three years into Mike Harris' renovated Ontario, with an election looming. The time seems right for a review. Let's see. Hospitals and schools are closing by the hundreds; thousands of former provincial employees are jobless; schools are in chaos; the Premier thinks a great place to meet pregnant welfare moms is the local beer store; Toronto the megacity is collapsing under the weight of its own amalgamated administration; the Premier can't figure out why Mr. Silly wasn't short-listed for the Giller award; the rich are getting greater tax cuts while the province won't even spring to bury the homeless.

What can one do but laugh?

1

The Common Sense REVOLUTION

"I want it all, and I want it now!"

There's never been a political document in Ontario quite like the Common Sense Revolution, drafted by Mike Harris and his advisers, the so-called Whiz Kids, prior to the 1995 election that swept him into office. It's a statement of philosophy and ideology more dramatic than anything put out previously by any other party in this province, including previous Progressive Conservative administrations.*

Most everyone is aware by now of the basic principles contained in the Common Sense Revolution. Mike Harris campaigned on a platform of lower

---

* It even beats "The Bland Manifesto" of the Bill Davis government.

taxes, reduced spending, and a balanced budget. The document spelled out how provincial personal income taxes would be reduced by 30 per cent, and how this infusion of cash into our wallets would boost the economy and create jobs. The document also promised that this could be accomplished without "cuts to health care."*

Here are some of the other principles listed in The Common Sense Revolution that not everyone may be aware of:

- **Big cars and fast-living are good for Ontarians:** You have a right to drive on the province's major expressways without fear of namby-pamby speed limits. If God hadn't intended for you to drive at 150 km/h, he would never have invented fuel injection. To this end, we will eliminate photo radar vans as soon as we take office and instead put them into service as high-speed, radar gun drive-by assessment vehicles for recalculating property values in the city of Toronto and elsewhere.

- **You can never have enough:** Our tax cut pledge will insure that the more you make, the more you'll get to spend. (Don't worry about our surtax for people earning more than $50,000; that's

---

* Some have cited this as evidence that the Tories broke their promise, what with hospitals closings and lineups in emergency rooms, but in fact it was nothing more than a typo in the original document. What was actually promised was no cuts to "wealth care." A promise made, a promise kept.

just window-dressing. We're going to look after you. People earning far less will get less back in the tax cut plan, but let's face it, if they knew what to spend money on, wouldn't they be making more of it in the first place?) If this copy of the Common Sense Revolution did not come with an Audi brochure, please call your local PC office and we'll mail it to you.

- **Nobody works as hard as you do:** Everybody else out there is ripping you off. While you're reading this, worrying about your province's future, the teachers, the civil servants, the nurses, the jail guards, snowplow drivers, those folks who mail out the cheques for the Family Support Plan, probably have their feet up right now and are watching *Wheel of Fortune*. Why should they be living on easy street when you've got so much to worry about, like why Emilio the pool boy forgot to pull over the solar blanket yet again?

- **It's okay to run with scissors:** The days of government interference in your life are over. Shouldn't you have the right to do as you please? If you want to swim less than an hour after eating, shouldn't you have the right to? If you want to run with a sucker in your mouth, is it anybody's business? Want to eat fish on a plane? Golf in an electrical storm? Do it! And if you want to pay your employee less than you've already contracted to pay him, shouldn't you feel free to express yourself in that manner?

If you can charge a new tenant more than the current occupier of the apartment, isn't it time to get the old tenant out of there?

- **You can eat your dessert first:** Where is it written that you have to eat all your vegetables before digging into your Jell-O with Cool Whip? That's why we're going to give you a tax cut right away, *before* we have the deficit under control, before we've figured out how we're going to wring billions out of health and education without destroying them. We don't care that the Standard & Poors bond rating service isn't going to give us better marks than they gave those Rae spendthrifts. You want your dessert now, and no one's going to stop you from having it.

- **Voters are dumb enough to believe anything:** Not you, of course. In fact, we don't know how this one slipped in here.

- **The lineup at the public trough is over:** It's time people stopped counting on the state to make a living for them, unless of course you have made a career in politics, first as a trustee and then a school board director and then an MPP and finally as a premier, and have fixed it so that you have a whopping fat pension to set you up for life once you're booted out of office.

- **Young offenders need tough discipline:** Social misfits and petty criminals need a firm hand to get their lives back in order. Teenagers who think it's okay to roam the streets in gangs, beating up on people and robbing them, are in for a surprise. After spending time at a boot camp where they'll have their heads shaved, be put in uniform, denied life's simple pleasures, and forced to get up at the crack of dawn to run up and down steep hills while wearing backpacks filled with cement, they'll find that once they're re-introduced to society, they'll no longer be petty thieves. They will be skinhead serial killers.

- **Bring business to Ontario:** We have to get the word out that Ontario is open for business. One way to do this is send trade representatives around the world. To Japan, to Europe, and across the United States. Tell them Ontario is the greatest place in the world. A great place to live. Fantastic schools! (When we get back home, we can deny ever saying that last one.) And while we're at it, we should make John Sewell special envoy to the Falklands. The sooner we get him out of town the better.

- **Just because a person may (and we are stressing the "MAY" here) have had a sixth toe on his right foot at some time in his life, that's no reason to think he's a strange alien from the planet Fairway, where the only time creatures ever feel compassion for one another is when they miss a six-inch putt:** We don't know how this one got in here, either. There's still a bit of editing to be done on this document.

■ The Whiz Kids

Those with the greatest influence on Mike Harris are the least seen. These are the folks who've come to be known as the Whiz Kids, a group of young members of the Tory party with a strong vision of where the party needs to be going. They're credited with being the architects of the Common Sense Revolution, and are huddled with the Premier on a nearly daily basis, holding breakfast meetings together and tucking him in at night, mapping out strategy for the Tories' re-election campaign.

But who are these Whiz Kids? Here are a few mini-profiles on the political geniuses who are reshaping your province:

- **Tiffany, age 6:** Tiffany is a lovely little girl whose political philosophy is already fully developed. She can sum it up in one word: "Mine!" Although sometimes she does it in two: "Mine! Mine!"

- **Bruno, age 9:** A charming youngster who often goes by his school yard nickname, "The Enforcer," Bruno is a master at dealing with those annoying special interest kids, like the ones with inhalers who claim they're unable to do sports. Bruno is skilled in persuading small children to stick their tongues to frozen bike racks, giving wedgies, putting firecrackers in frogs, and, during the summer months, kicking sand so skilfully into the faces of smaller children that it makes you wish it were an Olympic sport.

- **Biff, age 7:** What makes Biff stand out from his colleagues is a talent for applying simplistic solutions to tremendously complicated problems. For example, at the Common Sense Science Fair, the Whiz Kids were given the following puzzle to solve: It's tricky enough to build a ship in a bottle, but how does one get it back out? Biff claimed first prize for his innovative solution to this delicate problem, although he nearly lost a couple of marks when his sledge hammer kneecapped several of his teammates.

- **Randy, age 10:** When Mike Harris was putting together his team of young ideologues, he wanted someone with just the right kind of listening skills. When he was on a visit to a public school to observe a Grade 4 class, he couldn't help but be impressed with young Randy. The teacher said to him: "Randy, perhaps you could help us with the answer to this question." Randy doodled in his notebook. "Randy, excuse me? Do we have your full attention? I asked you a question." Randy began to engage in some serious booger mining and hit paydirt. Whoa! The size of this thing! "RANDY, DO YOU HEAR ME? EARTH TO RANDY!" the teacher bellowed. Young Randy was oblivious to his teacher's protests, her jumping up and down, her waving of notebooks in his face. This, the Premier concluded, was the kind of listening skills the Tory party needed.

2

What the TAX CUT Means to You

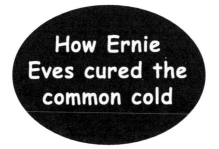

How Ernie Eves cured the common cold

One of the cornerstones of the Mike Harris Common Sense Revolution has been the 30 per cent cut in provincial income taxes. During the successful 1995 election campaign, the Tories said the economy needed a shot in the arm, and that shot would come in the form of a tax cut.

Here was the theory: When people have more money in their pocket, they spend it, which means more money ends up in the pockets of other people. Pretty soon, everybody's putting their fingers into everybody else's pockets and wiggling them around, and before you know it, you've got yourself an episode of *Melrose Place*.

Now, the way to achieve a tax cut is by reducing the size of the provincial budget, and the best way to reduce the size of the provincial budget is by reducing the size of the provincial government. Salaries generally account for the largest portion of any government's costs. The best way to hack away at salaries is to hack away at the number of employees.

The more people you fire, the more money you save. The more money you save, the greater tax cut you'll be able to provide. It's just that simple. If a way could be found to lay off everyone, your tax cut would be enormous.*

This is the way to a better, more prosperous Ontario. The more civil servants whose lives are brightened with a pink slip, the better your chance of getting a new freezer.

What everyone wants to know, of course, is this: How much am *I* going to get back? What is the value of *my* tax cut? And when you consider that there are going to be hikes in property taxes, new user fees, and soaring tuition costs, what is my net gain likely to be?

The following chart helps explain how much you'll be getting back once the Harris Tories finish with their tax cuts.

---

* Not to worry; the Tories are working on it.

INCOME GROUP	INCREASED BUYING POWER, on a weekly basis, after taking into account down-loading, user fees, etc.
Less than $15,150	2 Timbits
$15,150–$28,610	2 Timbits, one coffee (small)
$28,160–$44,890	1 donut six-pack, 2 coffees, 1 tea
$44,890–$54,000	1 dozen donuts, 6 coffees, 1 fritter
More than $100,000	Dinner for four at Scaramouche
More than $200,000	Buy your own donut franchise

■ How the Tories still find money for things

Some people are baffled by how this government, at a time when it's slashing spending while simultaneously cutting taxes, can still find money for any initiatives whatsoever.

For example, let's take a week where, on the Monday, the minister of transportation decides to spend $2 million to upgrade highway signs. Then, on Tuesday, the minister of health announces she's committing $2 million to buy new x-ray equipment. And two days later, on Thursday, the minister of community and social services manages to find $2 million, supposedly to create more daycare spaces.

Could it be that the Tories actually care about

some of these things? Are they a party that's sincerely interested in something besides the bottom line? Do they believe they have a role to play in improving the quality of life in this province for people other than those who live on streets with names like Honeysuckle Woodlawn Drive?

If the answer's yes, where are they getting the money?

Simple. Remember that list of $2 million announcements we just described?* It's the same $2 million.

In a garage deep beneath Queen's Park the Tories keep the Money Wagon.** Basically a dump truck, this is the vehicle that's dispatched to any funding announcement.

Say the education minister wants to announce out front of a school that there's another $2 million for textbooks. This is always a good photo-op. There's nothing the members of a school staff in this province enjoy more than having their picture taken with the education minister or a local Tory MPP, especially if they can extend their middle fingers just as the shutter's being snapped.

Anyway, a call is put in the day before any such announcement for the Money Wagon, so that it can be parked just behind the minister, in front of

---

* Sorry. We don't mean to insult you by suggesting you've got a short-term memory problem, but we have to accept that some Tories might read this book.

** It's parked right next to the Bat-Cart.

the school, where the cameras will be sure to catch it. Bundles of cash are seen close to overflowing in the payload area of the truck, held in place only by a clear plastic tarp.

If the minister of culture is making an announcement that the government is committing $2 million for the creation of a new opera centre, the truck is hauled out of the garage and raced to the theatre site, where a fat lady sits on the money pile and sings "Salome" by Richard Strauss.*

This helps explain why the Tories stagger their funding announcements. You can't have the truck with the two million buckaroonies in two places at once. Traditionally, announcements are spaced a day or two apart, unless they happen to be in the same town, in which case they can be handled on the same day, provided the truck doesn't get held up in traffic.

We decided to ride with Gus Whimple, Money Wagon driver, as he went about his duties the other day.

"You picked a good time to come," he said. "I've been busier than a Buffalo pharmacist dispensing north-of-the-border Viagra prescriptions. That's the way it seems to be as we get closer to an election. 'Get the truck! Get the truck!' It's all I hear these days. I'm whipped."

---

* In this version, instead of singing to the severed head of John the Baptist, it's Buzz Hargrove.

Whimple was eager to show me his rig. We crawled up on top of the load, pulled off the plastic tarp, and sat right in the cash.

"Pretty cool, eh?" he said. "But here's the really neat thing." He started digging down into the money, only a few inches, when he hit something with his hand. He knocked a couple of times, producing a hollow sound.

"False bottom," he said. "The cargo area's about six feet deep, but there's only about two inches of money. Not only does it save the government a fortune, it means the truck gets better mileage."

■ No gain without pain

Seeing as how thousands upon thousands of people — nurses, teachers, civil service workers — must lose their jobs so you can get your tax cut, it's only common decency to go about eliminating these jobs in the most humane way possible.

Any employee's supervisor who's entrusted with breaking the bad news should receive proper training. There's a right way and a wrong way to tell someone that he's about to be tossed out onto the street.

WRONG WAY:

"Well, Smithers, it's a heck of a thing, and I certainly hate to be the one to have to tell you this, but as it turns out, well, our budget isn't what it used to be since the province started its massive cuts, so I'm afraid we're going to have to let you go."

"Smithers, I have some bad news and I have some good news. The bad news is, well, we have to let you go. The province has slashed our department's budget, and we're having to lay off half the staff, and I can't tell you how sorry I am. But the good news is, I've bought a new camera with my tax cut! Check out this autofocus lens! Zooms in, zooms out, all by itself! It is *so* cool."

This way, the employee understands that there's a reason for his firing; that it's all part of a greater good.* Even though it may now be impossible to provide his family shelter, the fired employee gains a sense of fulfillment knowing his sacrifice will bring about a boom in the electronic gadget industry.

■ How the tax cut has brought prosperity to Ontario

The amazing thing about the tax cut is how it has created so many jobs, even before it's been fully implemented! Just the very *idea* of pending tax cuts has single-handedly kickstarted the Ontario economy, even though everyone on Bay Street, where you can find plenty of friends of the Harris government, say that a rebounding U.S. economy

---

* See Common Sense Revolution, Chapter 8, paragraph 9: "Let us not forget the words of Spock in *Star Trek II: The Wrath of Khan*. 'The needs of the many outweigh the needs of the few.' "

and lower interest rates, not the tax cut, are what's driving this province's recovery.

These Bay Street types are normally pretty good friends of the Tories, but some days they can be real poops. The government understands that even guys who live and breathe finance can, once in a while, have a bit of a blind spot. For example, Tories wonder why the *Globe and Mail* hasn't done any editorials about the explosion of jobs in the food bank and panhandling sectors. Why aren't this government's successes being recognized? The growth of panhandling, in particular, shows how things have picked up for the independent businessman.

The government has committed Money Wagon load after Money Wagon load (and we are not talking about those loads with the false bottoms) to getting their case across to Bay Street and everyone else in the province. The Tories have bought radio, TV, and newspaper ads to spread the word that Ontario is an island, a financial oasis, that can pull itself up by its bootstraps without help from anywhere else. These totally non-partisan ads point out how every new job in Ontario can be traced back to the tax cut. (Sample radio ad: "Ontario has 341,000 net new private sector jobs, no thanks to those Liberal and NDP dickheads.")

So confident is Finance Minister Ernie Eves of the power of the Tory tax cut that he bought air time on Ontario television stations to trumpet his

accomplishments. Inspired by the Premier's performance in an infomercial bragging about the position the province's schools have been placed in thanks to government intervention (in case you missed it, the show was called *Jeopardy!*).*
Eves decided to go straight to the people, rather than allow a biased media to filter and distort the message.

The show went something like this:

Eves: Good evening, and welcome to The Tax Party Pyramid, the game show about the Tory tax cut that allows viewers at home to play along with our studio guests. I'm your host, Ernie Eves, and I'd just like to ask our contestants one question. Are you ready to play Tax Party Pyramid?

Contestants: *(squealing)* Oh yes, yes!

Ernie: I'd like to welcome our players, David Tsubouchi, John Snobelen, Janet Ecker, and Elizabeth Witmer, to the show, and briefly explain the rules. You'll be divided into two teams, trying to identify an overall category with clues — a list of items from the category — that your partner gives you. Are we ready?

Contestants: You betcha.

Ernie: *(handing a card to John Snobelen, who is partnered with Janet Ecker)* Okay, John, you can

---

* The Tories sometimes broadcast these infomercials on their own network, CBLT (Can't Believe Lying Tories).

see the category on your card there, but now you have to give examples to Janet to see if she can guess it. And the clock starts . . . NOW!

Snobelen: A boost to the economy . . . more money in your pocket . . .

Ecker: Uh, things involving money. Things people talk about.

Snobelen: *(shaking his head no)* . . . A new VCR . . . a new vacation . . .

Ecker: Things you book! Things you shop for!

Snobelen: *(still shaking his head)* . . . a sunny day . . . a smile on a child's face . . . a week without rain . . . finding out your in-laws really can't come this weekend . . . warm socks right out of the dryer . . . the end of all human suffering as we know it . . . a cure for the common cold . . .

Ecker: Oh! Oh! I've got it! Things caused by the tax cut!

DING DING DING DING!

Ernie: Yes! "Things Caused By The Tax Cut" was the category. You just made it under the wire. Alright, Elizabeth, here's your card, and the clock starts . . . NOW!

Witmer: Poor children going hungry . . . adult education classes cancelled . . . huge lineups in emergency rooms . . .

Tsubouchi: Oh! Things that make you laugh!

Witmer: *(shaking her head, moving forward)* . . . two-year delays to hear cases at the Ontario Human Rights Commission . . . shortages of nurses . . . seven-year waits at the Adoption Disclosure Register . . . new user fees . . .

Tsubouchi: Oh! Oh! Things that you and I don't have to worry about!

Witmer: *(shaking head furiously)* . . . cancellation of French immersion busing . . . polarization between income groups . . . people sleeping on subway grates . . .

Tsubouchi: Oh! Things caused by El Niño!

DING DING DING DING!

Ernie: Whoa! For a minute there, I didn't think you were gonna get it, David, but you came through just before the bell. Excellent clues, Elizabeth! Hey, that's all for now, we'll be back after this paid political announcement!

MEMO #342087

To: All Relevant Ministries
From: The Office of the Premier

Re: Provincial Employee Appreciation

Given that morale among provincial employees, and not just those employed directly by the province, like ministry of transportation workers, but those indirectly employed by the government, like teachers for boards of education, is said to be at an all-time low, I believe it's time to recognize the good work they do, particularly in a time of cutbacks, which have really taken their toll.

To this end, I am proclaiming October ''Provincial Employee Appreciation Month.'' Please be on the lookout for future bulletins, which will list all the special activities.

Mike

3

The Environment:

If There's a Good One for Business, Everything Else Will Look After Itself

> **If bears and chipmunks don't pay taxes, how much protection are they due?**

We take you behind-the-scenes for a glimpse of what really goes on when Mike Harris meets with the members of his cabinet. On this particular occasion, a special meeting has been called to discuss some clear and immediate threats to the environment. Despite what some critics have charged, the Tories are very concerned about the quality of this province's air, lakes, and streams, and are ever vigilant to maintain the quality of life for every Ontario resident, little furry animal, and plant.

As the meeting gets underway, Harris attempts to get everyone in a relaxed mood by opening with a joke: The Premier has always considered himself a stand-up guy.

Premier: So this guy, he's a wildlife inspector or something, right? And he's coming through the woods and he comes upon this other guy who's made a campfire, and the wildlife inspector can tell right away that the guy is cooking a peregrine falcon for his dinner. So the wildlife inspector goes nuts, says he's going to have to arrest him, that the peregrine falcon is protected, right? But the guy says he hasn't eaten in days, and he was only trying to keep himself alive, and can't you give a guy a break, so the wildlife inspector cuts him some slack. And while the guy's eating the falcon, the wildlife fella asks, what does that taste like, anyway? And the guy says, it tastes a lot like bald eagle! Is that a knee-slapper or what?

Minister of Environment: That's a good one. But don't you remember? I told you that one last week, at the clubhouse, when I was giving you a hard time about taking 15 mulligans, and running over that Canada Goose with the golf cart?

Premier: I thought you knew that we never discuss my mulligans in the confines of this room, Norm. Do you understand?

Minister of Environment: Sorry, Mike, I forgot.

Premier: And when we're in these meetings, it's Mr. Premier. Are we clear? Anyway, I called this meeting to discuss what I believe is nothing short of an environmental crisis. On several fronts, this province's ecological stability is under attack, and we can no longer be complacent. We need a

strategy, an overall plan. First of all, do we have that report from the finance minister?

Minister of Finance: Here, Mr. Premier.

Premier: What did you find out with regard to the inhabitants of the provincial forestry reserves? The bears, the deer, the raccoons, the foxes. The whole lot of them.

Minister of Finance: Well, it's just as you suspected, Mr. Premier. None of them pay taxes. Not even a single field mouse. They're a drain on the provincial economy, and some of the craftier ones even know how to pry the lids off garbage cans. They're nothing short of squeegee rodents.

Premier: It's an outrage, no question. Here you and I are, busting our humps, making a living, paying taxes, while these so-called creatures of the forest scamper about without a care in the world. I think it's time we implemented FCVA.

Minister of Municipal Affairs: You mean CVA? Current Value Assessment?

Premier: No, I mean, FCVA, Forest Creature Value Assessment. Find out what these things are worth, by the pound, and tax accordingly. I'm sure any butcher could tell us the going rates.

Minister of Environment: Mr. Premier, we're getting creamed in the press over this latest report from the environmental commissioner and the medical association that our air quality is worse than ever.

Premier: Yeah, I've seen the papers. But any fool can tell you why the air's so bad. It's labour's fault.

Several ministers: Come again, Mr. Premier?

Premier: You ever driven by one of those strike sites, where they've set up their pickets? They've always got a fire going in a barrel, throwing in scraps of wood, putting loads of smoke into the air. Especially in winter, when strikers are trying to keep warm. That's why we have to clamp down on these unions, take away their right to strike, make them grateful to have a job at all. You got that?

Minister of Environment: Got it.

Premier: Now, how about the schools? I gather we've got a growing environmental disaster there.

Minister of Education: You'd be referring, of course, to the alarming presence of toxic mould in school portables.

Premier: Hell no. I don't know how that mould can hurt you when you can't even see it. I'm talking about green ribbons, you twit.

Minister of Education: The green ribbons?

Premier: Those things are poisoning the school atmosphere! They're emitting something, I don't know what, but it's getting into the minds of students and parents and teachers, and it's dangerous, let's not kid around here. It's affecting their brains, making them think strange thoughts, like there's something wrong with making every special education teacher a crossing guard. I want those ribbons eradicated.

Minister of Education: Suggestions?

Premier: I'd opt for spraying. I can never remember

what's banned and what's not banned, but if you could get a crop duster or something to take a buzz through school hallways, that ought to help. Whatever happened to DDT? Or Agent Orange? One of those ought to work.

Minister of Natural Resources: Mr. Premier, I'd like to direct your attention to the logging operation we've allowed to go ahead, where they're going to clearcut an area roughly the same size as Oklahoma. There've been a lot protesters up there, chaining themselves to the fences, lying down in the path of the trucks.

Premier: How many acres?

Minister of Natural Resources: A couple of billion, somewhere in there.

Premier: That's horrendous! Are you telling me that the trucks have to detour hundreds of miles to avoid where the protesters have set up?

Minister of Natural Resources: Yes, Mr. Premier.

Premier: Just think of the fossil fuels they're wasting as a result of those shenanigans. Think what all that extra exhaust is doing to the atmosphere! Would these be the same environmentalists who filed those access to information documents, wanting to know who the major polluters were? Do you know what kind of paperwork that caused? How many trees died to stall those folks in court, eh? Deal with it.

Minister of Education: Anything else, Mr. Premier?

Premier: I'd like to know how we're coming along with Lake Superior. Is it sold yet?

Minister of Natural Resources: Working on it.

Premier: Well, that about wraps it up, then. We've got a lot of work to do if we're going to make this province a safe environment for entrepreneurs to conduct their business without being harassed by tree-huggers and dirt-lovers. Is that a hand up I see? Yes, and who might you be?

Minister Without Portfolio Responsible for Seniors Issues: I'm the Minister Without Portfolio Responsible for Seniors Issues. Do you think there's a chance I could ever get a REAL cabinet job?

4

AMALGAMATION,
Just for the Fun of It!

Jobs available
for surgeons who
can prune trees

Bigger is better. Bigger is more efficient. Bigger is less wasteful. You've been hearing it forever and you heard it during all the *Godzilla* movie hype: Size does matter. (Maybe you saw some of the TTC buses redecorated during this period: "Mike Harris's list of enemies is as long as this bus.")

It's not surprising that a government comprised mostly of middle-aged white guys in suits (even Janet Ecker, Elizabeth Witmer, Dianne Cunningham, and other women in the Tory caucus are believed to be middle-aged white guys in suits wearing extremely clever disguises) think that if

something's bigger or longer, or both, well, that's got to be good.*

With this philosophical underpinning, the Tories have embarked on an amalgamation reign of terror. The list of things being amalgamated by the Harris Tories is huge. Among the things that have been merged, married, or lumped together — and in the process, often eliminated — are parks departments, hospitals, school boards, health units, entire cities, fire departments, municipal planning boards, even some provincial ridings. This has all been done in the name of efficiency, in the belief that bigger means less duplication, less waste, fewer staff, and, if you're a ratepayer, an eternity of being told to "Press 1" if you're trying to find out where to get a dog licence.

Consider the geography alone in some of these mergers. Twelve French language boards across the province were recently merged into one, now called District School Board Number 58. This board stretches from Gananoque to Sarnia, including Toronto, and north to Barrie. This is the only board where, if you want to make an appointment to see your trustee, you have to do it through Sunquest Tours.**

The Tories wanted to move as quickly as possible

---

* With the possible exception of welfare cheques and golf scores.

** The "58" refers to the number of light years it takes to get from one end of the board to the other.

on these mergers so that the cost savings would be evident before the next election. This meant moving with some haste.

Even the Tories will concede that it has not always been a smooth process. Some mergers have required a bit of tinkering after the fact. When you merge one agency with another, who runs the operation? When you combine two former ridings into one new one, which incumbent MPP gets to go before the voters next time around?

Some mergers were conducted so hurriedly one wonders how much thought went into them. A few of the amalgamations that raised eyebrows and caused the Tories to do a bit of rethinking include the following:

- **The Scarborough Parks Dept.–Women's College Hospital Merger:** "I have to admit," said Municipal Affairs Minister Al Leach at special hearings to discuss the melding of these two entities, "that on the face of it, it doesn't make a lot of sense, but just hear me out. That dingy old building, as the Premier has described it, will get a lot of sprucing up when responsibilities for its operation are in the hands of Wayne, the lawnmower guy. And there's no reason that nursing staff, between shifts, can't go out and spread some weed'n'feed around."

- **The Carleton Board of Education–City of North York Merger:** Students in the Ottawa area will no longer be taking familiar yellow school buses to classes, they'll be riding the new Sheppard subway line. And if there's any money left for theatre arts, kids will be mounting productions of *Sunset Boulevard*, *Show Boat*, and *Ragtime*, which recently completed their runs at a North York theatre. Also, with guidance from that city's former mayor, Mel Lastman, Carleton will be working to bring to its K-6 schools the 2006 Olympics, the next meeting of the G-7 leaders, and garish entertainment centres that allow you to experience, through the miracle of computer technology and virtual reality, what it feels like to make a complete fool of yourself.

- **City of East York–Doctor's Hospital–Etobicoke Fire Dept. Merger:** According to Tory government documents, this one came together because: "We just wanted to see if it could be done, and we loved the sound of it." There will be some job losses through this merger, but those employees who remain will, by necessity, hold a variety of skills. For example, there's currently an opening for a position described as "bylaw enforcement–heart surgeon–hose winder–upper officer." Interested applicants should have a firm grounding in parking meter strategies, surgical clamps, and have a high tolerance for flames. (If you are prone to asthma, you need not apply.)

- **The Teachers Federation–GTA Landfill Merger:** Under this Tory plan, teacher union leaders, including Earl Manners, Eileen Lennon, Marshall Jarvis, Phyllis Benedict, Maret Sadem-Thompson, and others will be bulldozed into oblivion at a new landfill site. (See also: The Ontario Federation of Labour–Mack Truck Bumper Merger.)

- **The Wellesley–Riverdale–St. Michael's–Pickering General–Salvation Army Toronto Grace–Whitby General–Oakville Trafalgar Memorial–Ottawa Civic Hospital Bedpan Merger:** Needless to say, this one's going to involve a lot of running around. Sharing one bedpan between eight hospital facilities will not only save the province a fortune in its bedpan budget, but will also keep workfare relay teams busy running the bedpan from facility to facility. (Cost of running shoes to be deducted from their workfare cheques.)

■ Birth of a megacity

While the creation of a megacity that would incorporate all the cities of Metropolitan Toronto is not something anyone remembers reading about in the 21-page Common Sense Revolution document, it became one of Mike Harris' priorities shortly after coming to office.

There were several reasons why the province decided to go ahead with Bill 103, The Mega-Arrogance Bill, which would turn Toronto, East York, York, Scarborough, Etobicoke, and North York into a single city, Toronto, not the least of which was traffic. The Premier, who hails from

North Bay and is not used to daily traffic chaos, had long complained about the time it took to get from one end of Metro to the other. He figured that if you only had to drive through one municipality instead of six, you could get around the city a heck of a lot faster.

The Tories had before them two exhaustive studies into the governance of the GTA (Greater Toronto Area).* The first, the Golden Report,** suggested that the administration of the six cities could be simplified if the Metro level, which oversaw the cities, were eliminated. Then there was the study by former Toronto mayor David Crombie, the "Who Sticks It To Whom" report, which recommended, among other things, that responsibility for welfare not be downloaded from the province onto the local level.

So in true Tory fashion, the province decided to do the opposite of what both reports recommended. It eliminated the six cities, and made municipalities everywhere responsible for welfare, social housing costs, and a host of other things, in exchange for the province taking over responsibility for education.

---

* After a court ruling permitted women to go about their business without wearing anything above the waist, GTA was amended to stand for Greater Topless Area.

** Initially quite popular with the Tories, who thought it had something to do with something you'd find in an ice-filled cooler after the 18th hole.

While combining the six city governments, and the existing Metro government, into one, the Harris government argued that huge administrative savings could be incurred, but best of all, the leftist loonies at Toronto council, particularly Mayor Barbara Hall, who let city workers join a day-long strike against the province, would be tossed out on their butts.

The Tories were caught a bit off-guard, however, by grass roots opposition to the megacity concept. So great was this opposition that referendums were held in each of the six cities, in which voters were asked if they'd like to put Mike Harris' head in a toilet and flush five times. The vote, known as "the swirlies plebiscite," was 76 per cent in favour. (Analysts said the vote might have been even higher had the plan called for one more flush.)

Despite those results, the Tories forged ahead with the megacity bill and created a huge council to oversee all of Toronto, stretching from the Mississauga line in the west to Pickering in the east and York Region in the north. Meetings now resemble opening night for a new *Star Wars* movie, except all the people crowding around aren't there to watch the meeting; they're the councillors.

This has led to some rough going at council meetings, as councillors from all areas of the city strive not only for consensus, but to be heard at all. In one such meeting, each councillor felt compelled to speak at length about a motion to adjourn for a washroom break. The vote came about three minutes too late, and those in the viewing gallery reported that it wasn't a pretty sight.

■ The Harris–Lastman battle

The war of words between new Toronto Mayor Mel Lastman and the Premier has erupted several times since the creation of the megacity. At one point, when the province appeared not to be living up to its part of the bargain of a revenue-neutral exchange of responsibilities with the city, leaving Toronto holding the bag for hundreds of millions of dollars, Mayor Mel went so far as to call Mike Harris "a liar," followed by something about his pants being on fire.

But the two men have patched things up for the most part. For example, in June, both agreed that it was a terrible thing that Geri, also known as Ginger Spice, was quitting the Spice Girls, although Mel took more direct action on this issue, sending special Spice Girl trauma teams into city schools to help pre-teen girls deal with the bad news.

The two men have managed not only to work together on some issues, but have even seen each other socially. One evening they even dined together, and everything went quite amicably until the bill arrived.

"Why don't we just split this down the middle," Mel suggested. "I know you had the swordfish, which cost twice what my entrée did, not that I even noticed, but what the hey, it's easier to add in the tip and divide the thing in half."

"Sounds good to me," said the Premier, just as the waitress arrived with their bill, which was for $160 million.

"It's pricey," Mel conceded, "but the service is good."

He was already looking through his wallet, glad that he had more than the usual number of thousand-dollar bills, while the Premier was still patting his back pockets, then his jacket.

"Gee, Mel, this is kind of embarrassing, but I think I left my wallet at the office."

"You did?"

"Heck of a thing. Listen, if you don't have enough cash, just put the meal on one of your cards, and I'll send you my half once I get to Queen's Park in the morning."

"Well, I guess," the mayor said, putting the whole thing on plastic.

The next morning, sitting in his office at City Hall, Lastman waited for the Premier to send over his part of the bill — $80 million plus tip. Before you knew it, it was the afternoon, and he still hadn't heard anything. He gave the Premier a call.

"Hey, uh, Mike, how ya doin'?"

"Great, Mel. What can I do you for?"

"Well, it's about last night? You know? You forgot your wallet?"

"Oh yeah! No probs! I'll have the money couriered over now." And he hung up.

Sure enough, within the hour, there was a courier at the mayor's office door dropping off an envelope. Mel peeked inside, and there it was: $10 million.

Hang on. Didn't the Premier owe him at least $70 million more? He got the Premier on the phone.

"Mike! The hell you doing to me?"

"Huh?"

"I just looked in the envelope here, and I'm $70 million short?"

"You are?"

"What the hell are you gonna do about it?"

There was silence on the other end of the line for a moment. Finally, Mike Harris said: "Well, because you're a good friend, I can spot you the $70 million."

"Say what?"

"I'll lend it to you. You're short $70 million, I'll give it to you, and just pay me back when you can."

The mayor thought about this. "Uh, I don't know, Mike. There's something fishy about this."

"I can hear the hesitation in your voice. Tell ya what. You only have to pay me back $50 million, and I won't charge any interest."

Whoa! Now that DID sound good. "Okay, Mikey, you've got yourself a deal."

When he got off the phone, Lastman leaned back

in his chair and lit himself a cigar. "I am one shrewd bargainer," he told himself.

■ Your very own personal sewage treatment plant

The downloading issue has gone hand-in-hand with amalgamation. The municipalities are now attempting to figure out how to handle financial responsibility for such things as welfare, and roads that used to belong to the province. Some cities and regions are finding that this trade-off of costs has actually left them worse off, contrary to the province's assurances of revenue-neutral deals.[*] Now, these same municipalities, in addition to raising property taxes, are having to do some downloading of their own.

The other day, there was a knock at the door, and when I answered it I found my local councillor standing there. He had in his hands a bucket, a shovel, and a very thick book.

"This is for you," he said. "See ya."

"Hang on," I said, taking the stuff into my arms. "What's this all about?"

"Read the manual," he said. "It's all in there."

The book was called "How To Run A Sewage Treatment Plant." There was a note, explaining that ratepayers throughout the city were being given responsibility for such things as water-

---

[*] Surprise!

57

mains, stretches of road, snow clearing, and hydro. I was now in charge of the local sewage treatment plant. Talk about drawing the short straw.

So now, every morning, before getting breakfast for the kids and heading off to work, I race on down to the plant, making sure everything's flowing through smoothly, that nothing's clogging up the works, and that all the environmental controls are in place. Things got a bit hairy back there in August, when I took a week off and couldn't get anyone to replace me. For seven days, if you flushed your toilet in Mimico, it bubbled up in somebody's house in Brampton.

Anyway, my wife won't sleep with me any more, and I've had to trade the Civic in for one of those Honey Wagons ("Please don't drop us off at school in that, Dad!" the kids plead, but deep down, I think they're proud of their old man). Now, when I hear people talking about all the shit they put up with from Mike Harris, I realize they drew the same assignment I did.

5

The Paint-by-Numbers
Approach to The Arts

"Disney could have saved
a ton if he'd just called
it 37 Dalmatians"

It's Thursday night, so it must be time again for a meeting of the Tory Book Club, organized by the Minister of Culture* to help change the image of the government's MPPs, cabinet ministers, and the Premier in particular, as a bunch of bone-headed, culturally illiterate, nincompoop Philistines who think the only good book is one that fits under a short table leg to keep it from wobbling.

---

* In the Tory regime, a cabinet posting on par with latrine orderly.

The culture minister has also been hoping to recast the government's reputation for seemingly caring little about the arts, a totally unfair conclusion. While it might be true that the Tories killed the Ontario Development Corporation and the Ontario Publishing Centre and hacked 40 per cent from the Ontario Arts Council, and mocked Coach House Press when it went under, wasn't it true that the Premier still enjoyed his painting hobby when relaxing up north? And did anyone even know, before Mike Harris was elected, that paint-by-number portraits of Jack Nicklaus existed?

Some of the early book club meetings were a bit awkward, because no one could figure out why the Tories had a minister of culture, given that they didn't give a rat's ass about culture. But considering that they also had ministers for education, labour, health, and the environment, and didn't give a rat's ass about any of those portfolios either, it seemed okay.

The Premier and each of his cabinet ministers were told to bring a book and be prepared to discuss it. Isabel Bassett, the culture minister, asked the Premier if he'd like to go first.

Looking a bit uncomfortable, he said: "Maybe someone else would like to talk about his or her book. I'm, uh, not quite ready yet."

"I could go," said Education Minister Dave Johnson. "I've been reading the Education Quality Improvement Act, you know, Bill 160, and I have to tell you, it's absolutely gripping."

"That's not exactly the sort of thing we're supposed to be reading for Tory Book Club," said Bassett. "We're supposed to be expanding our horizons by delving into literature, and fiction."

"Bill 160 is fiction," Johnson said in his defence. "Everything in it says it will make the education system better, but everyone knows that's just made up."

"Let's move on. How about you, Al?"

The Als (Palladini and Leach) said simultaneously: "Yes?"

Bassett nodded to the municipal affairs minister, Al Leach. "Every night, before I go to sleep, I read a little bit of the bill that merged all of Toronto into one big megacity. I know I should have done it before it went through, but I was busy, what with John Sewell dropping by the house all the time for tea. This bill's even better than the last Grisham thriller I read."*

The culture minister sighed. This just wasn't the way it was supposed to go. She thought she'd give someone else a try. The other Al.

"I know I'm not the transportation minister any more," Palladini said, "but the highway's in my blood, you know? That's why I've been reading The Official Driver's Handbook, published by the ministry. And it's right up our alley politically,

---

* This, actually, is a pretty believable statement.

outlining how dangerous a turn to the left can be."

The culture minister felt a bit like weeping. "Elizabeth," she said to Health Minister Witmer, "surely you've got some sort of report you could present to book club?"

"It's hard to beat the literature on the hospital restructuring act without getting all excited. Your blood starts to rush, your heart begins to pound. All this document needs on the cover is a drawing of Fabio."

Bassett decided to go back to her first victim. "Mr. Premier, are you ready?"

"Uh, okay, sure. As you know, I've been looking at the deeper meanings of *Mr. Silly*, which works, I think, on many levels. As a metaphor for one's life in public office, it stands as an allegorical statement that characterizes, through the use of imagery and alliteration —"

The culture minister held up her hand. "Excuse me, Mr. Premier, but are you reading that?"

"Oh no, these are my own thoughts."

"What's that you've got in your lap?" And she stepped around the table and grabbed a yellow and black booklet out of the Premier's hand.

"You ought to be ashamed of yourself," she said sternly. The Premier looked sheepish. "Going out and buying the Cole's Notes version of *Mr. Silly*."

"Okay, you caught me. But I just didn't have time to read the original. It's like, 24 pages or something. Where's the harm?"

"The Coles version is 10 times longer than the book itself! You either come to book club prepared to discuss what you've read, or you don't. Reading the Cole's Notes version is unacceptable!"

"I suppose you're right. I'm really sorry."

"I have a confession to make," said Johnson, slapping a yellow-and-black book on the desk. "I read the Cole's Notes version of Bill 160."

"Aw nuts," said Leach, tossing a similar book out onto the desk. "Same here. I got the Cole's Notes version of the act to amalgamate the city of Toronto."

Said Palladini: "Ditto. Cole's Notes for the driver's handbook."

"Well, I guess I might as well come clean, too," said Witmer, pulling a yellow-and-black book out of her purse. "I read the Cole's Notes version of the hospital restructuring act, too."

"I think I speak for all of us," the Premier said, "when I say that hey, who's got time to read all these new omnibus laws and massive bills and understand the ramifications of what we're doing? There's so much legislation coming so damn fast. How can we be expected to get a handle on the subtle nuances contained within them? And finally, when I want to read a little something for myself, like *Mr. Silly*, I don't even have time for that. Listen, without Cole's Notes, this cabinet would have no idea what it's doing."

■ Some of Mike Harris' Favourite Hardy Boy Adventures

When the Premier let it slip that one of his favourite books was *Mr. Silly*, he also mentioned that he was a fan of the Hardy Boys mystery series. The adventures of Frank and Joe had always been a great source of entertainment, he told reporters.*

There are a great many Hardy Boy books, but what follows is a partial list of some of the Premier's faves:

- **The Haunted Legislature:** Frank and Joe are called in to investigate reports of a ghostly apparition wandering the halls of Queen's Park. They begin to believe something that lived in this great building long ago met a horrible death, and now roams about aimlessly, hoping to reappear. (Also published under the title: "The Ghost of Democracy.")

- **The Great Amalgamation Mystery:** Frank and Joe are hot on the trail of the Revenue Neutral Gang, who've convinced several municipalities that if they merge, their savings will be enormous. But once the amalgamation's complete, the Revenue Neutral Gang rides off into the sunset with all the savings.

---

* The Premier, who prides himself on being really plugged in to Canadian literature, is said to be looking for a series of detective novels that feature a recurring character. "I'm wondering," he told reporters, "if anyone knows where I can get my hands on the Roe Hinton Mysteries."

- **The Disappearing Instructional Assistant:** Frank and Joe try to find out what's happened to all the teachers' assistants, who were there in the classroom one day helping disabled children, and the next day, were gone!

- **The Daycare Centre on the Cliff:** Who was at the controls of the bulldozer when the Trillium Subsidized Daycare Centre for Boys and Girls got shoved off the bluffs and into Lake Ontario? Frank and Joe are on the case!

- **The Secret of the Named Young Offender:** Frank and Joe are hired by a disgraced cabinet minister who wants to know who set him up to take the fall for the naming of a young offender in a Throne Speech! Frank and Joe's investigation leads them right to the top!

■ Movie Time!

In addition to his passion for fine literature, the Premier is also a great admirer of the cinema.

Most people think Harris was kidding when he said of his taste in movies: "I'm looking to be entertained, not to be taught anything." The fact is, Mike Harris thinks there's a lesson to be learned from many movies. Often, amazingly enough, it's a fiscal lesson.

And to hammer that lesson home, the Premier has established a companion agency to the Ontario Film Review Board, called the Ontario Film Fat

Board, that will rate movies according to their depiction of wastefulness.

The board will work something like this: It will give the film's current title, followed by the board's suggestion for an alternate title, with an explanation for its decision:

OLD FILM TITLE	NEW TITLE, with the Ontario Film Fat Board's suggested changes
The Ten Commandments	**The Seven Commandments:** In a time of decreased regulation and cutting red tape, who needs all those extra rules? If Moses can't get his message across in seven, he's just making things too complicated.
Snow White and the Seven Dwarfs	**Snow White and the Dwarf:** This Disney classic is marred by its obviously padded payroll. One dwarf can easily do the work of seven, especially when you consider the others have names like Sleepy, Dopey, uhh, Scary, Sporty, Baby, and Ginger. The other six will be encouraged to take an early retirement plan; it's hoped the jobs can be reduced through attrition. But if not, cut the little guys loose.
101 Dalmatians	**37 Dalmatians:** Another financially reckless Disney flick. No one needs to have that many dogs, although you can bet anyone who does probably buys the mutts their food with welfare bucks.

Four Weddings and a Funeral	**Three Weddings, No Funeral**: You got any idea what it costs to put on a wedding these days? A fortune, that's what! No movie needs four. We're being generous to allow three. As for the funeral, the budget's already blown, unless they put the deceased on an ice floe.
Seven Brides for Seven Brothers	**Four Brides for Four Brothers**: See above. At least there's no funeral.
The Three Musketeers	**The Musketeer**: The private sector has gone through incredible downsizing in recent years. Many people are now having to assume added responsibilities that were once those of their colleagues. Why should the swashbuckling industry be any different?
The Three Faces of Eve	**Eve, The Two-Faced Girl!**: Some producer somewhere should have had the guts to take Joanne Woodward aside and say: "You're only getting two faces, and that's it!"
The Dirty Dozen	**The Dirty Half-Dozen**: Do the math. Which costs less: a feature with a dozen big stars or just six? Let's face it, our idea of a great flick is something like *My Dinner with André*; two guys having dinner, no costly special effects, and it's so boring no one goes anyway, which means moviegoers have another eight bucks to put toward a snowmobile, which means more manufacturing jobs, and more work for search-and-rescue teams.

MEMO #342398
(Correction to Memo #342087)

To: All Relevant Ministries
From: The Office of the Premier

Re: Provincial Employee Appreciation

There's been a change to our announcement about making October ''Provincial Employee Appreciation Month.'' Rather than provide a list of activities at this time, as was earlier promised, I've decided a whole month honouring folks who work for the province is a bit extravagant at a time when we're having to trim our budgets a teensy bit.

''Provincial Employee Appreciation Month'' will now be called ''Provincial Employee Appreciation Week,'' and will be held starting Oct. 19. The objective remains the same: to show our workers that we still care deeply about the work they do. But there's no reason this message can't be communicated in a week instead of a month.

6

The Tories' Malpractice Approach to HEALTH CARE

Get your Do-It-Yourself Surgery Kit today!

Y ou know, worrying about all the disruptions brought about by the Common Sense Revolution can get you down after awhile. Sometimes the best thing to do is put it out of your mind for a period of time, find a distraction, have a little fun. And the best prescription for that can be taking a trip.

A vacation doesn't have to be expensive. You can often find a lot of fun in your own backyard, by which we mean your hometown. How many people who've lived in Toronto their whole lives, for example, never get around to visiting the CN Tower, or the Ontario Science Centre, or even venture into neighbourhoods other than their own? Say you grew up in what used to be known as Etobicoke. When's the last time you checked out Chinatown? Or the Beaches? If you grew up in downtown Toronto, when's the last time you ventured up Yonge St. to see the massive development in the North York area, with its new skyscrapers and theatres?

Okay, you say, I'm convinced! I want to see Hogtown! I want to see it like I've never seen it before, and I want to see it now! Give me the number of a travel agency who can make my dreams come true!

Got a pencil and paper? Write this down. For a tour of the big city, call 911.

When the operator answers and asks whether your call should be directed to the police, the fire department, or an ambulance dispatcher, say: "I'm in the mood for travel, so I'll take ambulance!"

Now, to get the most out of this trip, before the ambulance gets there, you're going to have to be ready. You might think that means throwing a few things into an overnight bag, but not this time. What you have to do now is come down with a serious ailment.

Your choices are endless. It can be chest pains, or failure to catch one's breath, even dizziness. You might want to throw yourself down the stairs.

Perhaps you can arrange to be bitten by the neighbour's rabid pitbull. Just make sure it isn't something weenie-like, say a bad rash or unwanted facial hair. The more serious your problem, the more of the city you're likely to see.

Once you've decided on your health problem, you're ready. When the ambulance attendant arrives, say something like: "Dear god, get me to the closest hospital, fast!" Then collapse.

From your spot in the back of the van, you'll hear the driver talking on the radio to his dispatcher.

"We're on our way to Scarborough General!" The ambulance takes off, siren wailing! This is what you'd hoped for! The siren! Weee-hawwww!

In a few moments, you feel the vehicle pulling into a driveway. There are bright lights, a white "H" on a blue background. The driver gets out. He's gone for quite some time. No one makes any move to take you out of the back of the ambulance. The vehicle idles.

Finally, the driver returns. "No beds here. We're being redirected."

And then you're off again, this time to a totally different part of the city! Vroom! The siren's on again!

Another driveway, another blue "H" sign. The driver disappears again. Then he's back. Off you go to another hospital. And then another, and then *another!* Strains of Willie Nelson crooning "On the road again!" whistle through your mind.

And on it goes, through the night. Before you

know it, you've travelled to York and East York, you've raced through Etobicoke, you've been from the northern reaches of North York and back down to the waterfront, searching for a facility with a bed. You've gotten a tour of the city unlike any you've ever had before!

One final note before planning a trip like this: All the other ambulances in the city are conducting similar tours, and they can go on for days. So book early!

■ Solving hospital overcrowding

Anyone who's read a newspaper or turned on the TV news in the last couple of years has become accustomed to hearing about patients stacked up in the hallways of Ontario hospitals. Just trying to maneuver down a hospital corridor when it's lined with double-parked gurneys, each one bearing a patient hooked up to an IV drip, has become an adventure in itself.

The province is well aware of this problem, and has pledged to do something about it. Just recently, the health minister committed millions of dollars to building more hallways.

Here's what she said in her press release: "This government is not going to sit idly by while this problem grows even worse. We have undertaken studies to determine why hospital hallways have become more crowded, and have come to the only logical conclusion; that the time has come to open up the purse strings and create more spaces for the sick, the elderly, the injured.

"That's why this ministry is undertaking a five-year program to add corridors to Ontario hospitals that need them. The spending breakdown is as follows:

Year One	Lots and lots of money
Year Two	Some more
Year Three	The same as Year Two
Year Four	A whole pile
Year Five	Ask Ernie

Never in the history of this province has there been this kind of commitment to restoring the quality of health care. We believe this approach will significantly decrease the number of patients per hallway." The health minister then showed some slides of hallway construction in a factory.

"These hallways can be assembled at a remote location, then shipped to whatever hospital requires them."

There was a comment from a member of the press. "Those hallways, they look a lot like school portables, only they're longer and skinnier."

"That's correct," the minister said. "We'll be ringing the hospitals with them, as many as they need."

"Aren't you worried that portable hallways will be prone to the same problem as portable classrooms? You know, toxic mould?"

The health minister smiled. "That's the beauty of it. If any of the patients being housed in our portable hallways should become infected with a deadly strain of mould, they're already at a hospital facility!"

Also, the minister said, in the interests of making lengthy waits in hospital emergency rooms more tolerable, admitting staffs are being instructed by the province to hand out to patients the following list:

THINGS TO DO WHILE WAITING IN EMERG

1. Read *War and Peace*.
2. Move on to *Moby Dick*.
3. Bring along a copy of the Common Sense Revolution and look for the place where they promised the week-long emergency room wait.
4. Come up with some exciting new tuna recipes.
5. Write a letter to Bob Rae saying all is forgiven.
6. Go to the pay phone, call the Family Support Plan to see where your cheque is, and stay on hold. It will be interesting to see who acknowledges you first: the nurse or the receptionist.
7. Wander through the hospital's west wing and empty some bedpans.
8. Figure how many hours of private nursing care you can buy with your tax cut.
9. Start making flyers for the Liberal or NDP candidate in your riding.
10. Bleed.

■ Preventive medicine and more

The Tories think preventive medicine — defined by them as preventing you from getting medical attention — can be expanded to include promoting a lifestyle that keeps admissions to a hospital facility to a minimum. This is a good idea that the Tories believe can be taken a step further.

That's why researchers within the ministry of health have been busy working on special self-help books that will be sent to every household in Ontario. Titled "Your Guide to Safe Do-It-Yourself Surgery," the booklet explains in simple, everyday language, how you can conduct many medical procedures on yourself that have become quite commonplace in a hospital setting.

"The fact is," the booklet explains, "many types of surgery have become so routine, it seems downright silly to have high-priced doctors charging exorbitant fees to OHIP for something you could do yourself, especially if you're handy with tools. Do you like to assemble things? Have you ever built your own deck? Resurfaced a driveway? You probably have all the skills you need.

"There are many advantages to do-it-yourself surgery. First of all, there is no waiting period. Nowadays, if you want heart surgery, you may wait months before there's an opening at the hospital.

Those waits are over! Plus, there's no annoying
trip to the hospital, no hanging around, no nurses
waking you up at 5:30 in the morning to give
you your breakfast. When you perform your own
surgery, in your own home, you can work at your
own pace, when you want, where you want. And
you can have your breakfast any old time you
please!

"Let's take something simple, like a tonsillec-
tomy. Here's what you're going to need:

- *Ice cream (not Rocky Road; you want something smooth going down)*

- *Bowl and spoon*

- *A mirror (bathroom vanity ideal — because
  you're going to need your hands free)*

- *Really really really really really sharp knife*

- *Needle and thread*

"There you have it! And to think, doctors get
paid big bucks to do this! Not only does Do-It-

Yourself Surgery allow the province to redirect funds to health care projects that are far more critical,* it gives you a sense of accomplishment. You'll be able to stand before your friends, point into your throat and say 'I did this!' assuming of course you have not swallowed too much of your own blood.

"Watch for our next exciting pamphlet: Do Your Own Vasectomy!"

■ Bringing in the private sector

One way to make the delivery of health care more efficient is to turn portions of it over to the private sector.

Delivery is the key word here. That's why the province has been holding behind-closed-doors sessions for several months now with major pizza conglomerates. Let's face it; we're a society that puts a higher value on the speedy delivery of food than the quick and efficient delivery of medical attention. Why not turn to the experts for advice?

This is a consumer-driven decision. People expect their food delivered fast, and hot. Let's say you've been promised a double-cheese and pepperoni pizza at your door in 30 minutes, but now it's been more than 45. You pick up the phone and you say:

---

* Like rubber surgical tubing for beating people who try to use bogus health cards.

"Listen, pal, that pizza was supposed to be here in half an hour and it's late and I want to know what the hell you're going to do about it!"

Compare this to being told by your doctor that, while your body is harbouring a tumour the size of a grapefruit that will soon devour your intestines whole, there's a better chance Preston Manning will he hired to do the voice of Darth Vader in the new *Star Wars* movies before a bed becomes available in your local cash-strapped hospital. You get on the phone and say:

"Oh well, I guess that's the way things are these days."

An operation may soon be no more than a phone call away. Let's say you and your spouse and two children are home on a Friday night, and you're experiencing terrible chest pains while everyone else is starving. Phone that seven-digit number you know so well from the radio jingles and order two medium pizzas with everything, three Cokes, and a triple-valve replacement. It'll be at your door in minutes!

Soon we can turn the court system over to the fast-food folks. No more ridiculous postponements from defence lawyers. No jury deliberations to exceed 30 minutes.

◼ Closing hospitals

In the lead-up to the last election, Premier Mike Harris made it clear that closing hospitals was not part of his plan. And in fact, it isn't. Many community hospitals that once offered a wide range of medical services may stop tending to the sick, but that's no reason the building itself has to be mothballed. There are many alternative uses.

Already, former hospitals are being converted into other needed services for the citizens of Ontario. Coming soon to a former medical facility near you: The David Tsubouchi Cooking School (this will actually be an entire chain offering lessons into how to make tinned seafood a dining adventure), OPP Riot Squad Discount Fashion Outlet (featuring everything from helmets and boots to clubs; super for the fetish crowd), pro shops, and supply centres for people in the squeegee and panhandling industries.

◼ A word about nurses

The province's nurses would have you believe that these are pretty tough times for them, what with their increased workload, fewer colleagues (10,000 fewer since the beginning of this decade) to help them, and a general lack of respect from the province.

At a time when the Tories are supposedly committed to saving money across the board in health care, they backed down in what you might call a major area — physicians' salaries. The Tories eliminated clawbacks and allowed the Ontario Medical Association a 1.5 per cent annual overall increase in fees over three years. Allowing doctors a raise while attempting to cut health care costs is a bit like getting tough with sharks by tossing them more people to eat.

The nurses could have wangled a deal like this too and kept their profession from being decimated if they'd only been better at networking. If you want to get along with Tories, you have to hang out with Tories. You have to golf with them. You have to go to the club with them. You have to go hunting with them. You have to drive a Lexus so you'll run into one when you're getting the oil changed. You have to hang out in the same restaurants.

The doctors understood this.

Once nurses understand that there's a lot to be gained by inviting cabinet ministers up to their cottages on Lake Rosseau, their lot's bound to improve.*

---

* Ditto welfare moms.

7

It's a CRIME What the Tories Are Doing

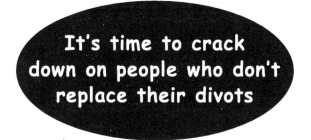

It's time to crack down on people who don't replace their divots

Before you read another word, go bolt your door. Slip on the chain. Pull back the curtain and have a look at who may be lurking about on the street. Turn on the front and back porch lights. If you have to go out for the evening, set the timer lights. Call in a security expert. Install motion detectors. Have your home wired into a centralized alarm network. Consider hiring your own personal bodyguard. You must take every precaution possible, because you never know when a notorious Tory crime fighter will try to burst through your door to scare the bejeesus out of you.

From Mike Harris' perspective, there's nothing

better than a scared electorate. If you're scared, chances are when the next election rolls around you'll cast your vote for the party that wants to get tough with criminals. And the party that wants to get tough with criminals is the party that will try to scare you the most.

At your local all-candidates meeting in the next provincial election, expect exchanges like this:

Tory Candidate: Just ask my opponent his record on stiffer penalties for serial killers who laser beam their victims to death. I say string them up! But what does my opponent think? Who knows! He's never so much as said a single word on the issue!

Liberal Candidate: Uh, to my knowledge there never have been any serial killers who use laser beams in the commission of their crimes.

Tory Candidate: Is this what you want, people? A representative who hasn't considered all the alternatives? And I promise you right now, I will not support a laser gun registry like my friend here no doubt does. Laser beams don't kill people; people kill people.

It's no surprise the Tories have chosen to ignore recent studies showing the crime rate going down. It doesn't serve their interests, or play to their constituencies. This, after all, is a government that's so determined to discredit and dismantle the education system that it pretended not to notice when Durham Region's Sinclair Secondary School won a prestigious international award for excellence. Why didn't the minister run out there for a photo op? There's no political gain in recognizing outstanding achievement in schools, or admitting that there's a drop in the crime rate.

To gauge* public concerns about crime, the Tories established a commission that wandered the province holding hearings, often getting to them in record time because they didn't have to be on the look-out for photo radar vans. In an effort to boost awareness about crime, and attendance, at these hearings, special advance teams went into communities where hearings were to be held to stir up interest. These teams consisted of boot camp inmates whose assignments were to break windows, slash tires, frighten little old ladies, and cross against the lights.

After several months of hearings, here are the recommendations of the Ontario Crime Control and Electric Chair Commission:

- New Democrat MPPs like Peter Kormos must get 10 years for exposing inefficiencies in the offices of the Family Support Plan, even if the courts do find him not guilty.

- Picketing without a licence warrants a sentence of 18 months to two years.

---

* Read "mold."

- Anyone who leaks Tory re-election strategy documents receives a term of no less than life imprisonment.

- You get 1–2 weeks in jail for not replacing your divot.

- The parents of labour leaders will be held responsible for wage hikes their children negotiate with their unions' employers.

- First-time young offenders should be dealt with by the community through a special lynching program.

- It's time to bring back the strap for any teacher participating in a political walkout.

- Prison counsellors and social workers will be replaced by members of the OPP riot squad.

- Lower the age for charging young offenders to six months.

- Welfare recipients must wear a scarlet "W" stitched to their shirts.

Among those troublemakers the Premier particularly wants to crack down on are argumentative backbench MPPs. These are the party members who have not always towed the line when it comes to Tory policy. People like Gary Carr, from Oakville South, Bill Murdoch, from Grey–Owen Sound, and Toni Skarica, from Wentworth North, who've raised questions about such decisions as downloading various costs onto municipalities.

To the Premier's mind, there's no greater crime for one of his people to commit than that of independent thinking. These MPPs are generally shipped off to backbench boot camp where they watch training films consisting of Elizabeth Witmer interviews on Focus Ontario, where she can speak for 30 minutes without answering a single one of Robert Fisher's questions.

■ How special are you?

One of the things the Tories have championed is fingerprinting. We already fingerprint criminal suspects upon their arrest, but the Tories want to go further. For example, their endorsement of a plan to fingerprint welfare recipients sparked a heated debate between those who thought it was a good way to eliminate fraud, and those who said it equated receiving welfare with a criminal act, which, of course, it is.*

But now the Mike Harris government is seeking to fingerprint more citizens of Ontario; namely, all members of special interest groups.

If you're part of a special interest group, you'll soon be receiving in the mail a notice from the province telling you when and where to be finger-

---

* Common Sense Revolution, chapter 2, paragraph 4, clause (b): "And we will move to make cashing a welfare cheque a crime punishable by 10 swats of this document, rolled up like a newspaper."

printed. Be sure to save this card! If you don't have it with you when you go to your fingerprinting station, you'll be subjected to a full body cavity search by a randomly selected cabinet minister who may or may not be wearing gloves.

But what do you do if you think you should receive a fingerprinting card but do not? How can you determine whether you're part of a special interest group?

Let's see. A special interest is defined by the Harris administration as any person, organization, or informal group who disagrees with anything the Tories do. For example, let's say you have your flicker on indicating that you've got dibs on a parking space someone's pulling out of. Just as the car backs out, another car approaches and whips into the spot you've been waiting for. You roll down your window to tell the other driver, as he gets out of his car, that he swiped your spot. If this person is the Premier, he will point at you and scream: "Special interest!"

But maybe you don't drive and this example is not very helpful. So we've put together a more comprehensive list, although, admittedly, it's far from complete.

If you fit into any of the categories on the following page, watch for your notice in the mail!

ARE YOU ON THE OFFICIAL MIKE HARRIS SPECIAL INTEREST HIT LIST?

Welfare recipients, labour leaders, doctors, nurses, municipal employees, students, parents, union members, squeegee kids, teachers, principals, vice-principals, OPSEU members, Leah Casselman, 416 mayors, 905 mayors, every single last citizen of the former Metro Toronto, Tory backbenchers, mothers who no longer know how to make hot porridge, the Iraqis, the Iranians, separatist hospital administrators, hula-hoop makers, school board trustees, gambling opponents, refugees, the sick, the elderly, artists, parents who wouldn't let their children participate in Grade 3 testing, beer-guzzling welfare moms, Chris Stockwell, members of the Liberal party of Ontario, members of the New Democratic Party of Ontario, people with opposable thumbs, the surviving Dionne Quintuplets, the Bread Not Circuses activist group, injured workers, tenants, children's aid society clients, editorialists, junior kindergarten students, the poor, special education students, impatient golfers who want to play through, gun registry proponents, hospital workers, Jean Chrétien, Paul Martin, gays and lesbians, topless women, all other women, the homeless, people who wear green ribbons and, finally, Ontarians who still think democracy is a concept worth preserving.

■ Boot Camps

When the Tories first began to think about solving the crime problem, they were faced with a choice in philosophies. Did they want to address a child's formative years, taking the long view that a person may be deterred from a life of crime by having a supportive school system, perhaps junior kindergarten, well-funded children's aid societies that can respond promptly to help a child in crisis, a strong social safety net that offers adequate child care, and a generally caring environment for the next generation? Or did they just want to beat the crap out of kids today who misbehave?

The Tories chose the latter.

This led to the establishment of boot camps to deal with tough, young lawbreakers. These camps were modelled on the chain gang programs in the U.S., in which inmates are used to pick up trash from the roadside. But because Canadians don't have as bad a reputation for littering as their neighbours to the south, some adjustments had to be made. Before boot camp programs could begin, welfare recipients on workfare had to be dispatched across the province, with bags full of litter, so that Ontario highways could be readied. (People who think the workfare program is a waste of time are usually put in their place when they hear this story.)

Eager to make sure the boot camps were run properly, the Harris government hired as consultants people who had penned the scripts for such films as *Cool Hand Luke*, *The Shawshank Redemption*, and *Brubaker*. Then, to ensure that the first boot camp was as authentic as possible, the ministry of corrections made sure that 95 per cent of the inmates were actors, who could coach the other 5 per cent on how to perform like real badass delinquents. For example, one of the first people sent to a provincial boot camp was Winona Sylvester, 68, of Walkerton, Ont., who was convicted of keeping too many cats in her house. Whenever camp officials wanted her to badmouth them or set a cot on fire to show how she needed to be kept in line, all she wanted to do was open up a fresh bag of kitty litter.

Anyway, the official opening of the first boot camp proved to be a bit of an embarrassment for Solicitor-General Bob Runciman, who arrived just after two inmates escaped, during a power failure, in a stolen van. While this may have looked bad, the two escapees were, in fact, among the ministry-hired actors, on their way to Toronto for a *Cats* audition.

■ Watch for the Premier's memoirs

Although it might have sounded like something the Tories would have supported, privately the Premier and his cabinet were relieved that federal Liberal MP Tom Wappel's Bill C-220 to keep menaces to society from writing about their exploits, and profiting from it, was killed in the Senate.

This was a popular cause among the loonie right, who railed on about the likes of Karla Homolka and Clifford Olson making a fortune by writing their life stories, even though neither Karla Homolka nor Clifford Olson had book deals, and no publisher wanted to offer such book deals, except for publishers who are eager to have their offices firebombed. Although Wappel's bill managed to get through the House of Commons, it bogged down in the Senate, which evidently listened to such groups as the Writers' Union of Canada, which pointed out that books like Kirk Makin's *Redrum The Innocent* that helped overturn the conviction of Guy Paul Morin, would never have been written under a law like this.

This bill to muzzle folks with a record of mayhem and destruction was viewed with considerable alarm by members of the Tory cabinet who, once their current term of employment ends after the next election, want to write about what they did while in office. Now Mike Harris can write his memoirs without fear of being stripped of his royalties.

8

The UNITY CRISIS: Leading the Way

How the Calgary Declaration is a lot like the stampede

Ontario has a long tradition of leading the way when it comes to looking for solutions to the national unity crisis. While the Meech Lake Accord and the Charlottetown Agreement failed to bring Quebec into the constitutional fold, at least the various premiers of Ontario over the last decade have been front and centre at the negotiating table, searching for compromise, desperate to find ways to open the lines of dialogue.

Now, in the tradition of Bob Rae, and before him, David Peterson, Mike Harris is committed to making his mark, to having a presence on the national scene. Back in 1996, the Premier showed he'd been doing his homework on the issue, when he told a group of businessmen in Manhattan that there was no chance, "zilch, absolutely zero," that Quebec would ever separate from Canada. This conclusion came as quite a surprise to many people.*

The Premier is reportedly always ready during caucus meetings to enter into a debate about the future of this country, and Quebec's place in it. Here's a typical exchange:

Backbench MPP: Uh, Mr. Premier, just what is Ontario's position with regard to Quebec. Are we going to stick by the deal worked out in Calgary?

Premier: I will not back down on the 30 per cent tax cut for Ontarians.

MPP: No, no, I was wondering about the so-called Calgary Declaration, and Quebec?

Premier: I'm going to eliminate the deficit! Stick it to welfare recipients! Stick it to teachers! Get their pension fund! Man, we gotta get a piece of that!

MPP: Quebec, sir?

Premier: Well, I sure love that *Just for Laughs* show they do from Montreal.

Wisely, the Premier decided to make someone within the Cabinet responsible for the Quebec issue. This may help explain why you've never

---

* For example, those who read newspapers and watch *The National.*

heard of Dianne Cunningham. The Premier picked her.

Cunningham decided that perhaps the best way to determine how the province should move on national unity was to ascertain how the average Ontarian felt about the issue. She wondered, hesitantly, how the Premier might feel about going straight to the people for an opinion. She was well aware that on many issues the Premier did what he wanted, regardless of how voters seemed to be thinking.

When Metro Toronto voted overwhelmingly against the megacity concept, for example, the Premier didn't pay any attention to the result. Despite municipal plebiscites on gambling that were strongly opposed to the establishment of more casinos or video lottery terminals, the Premier chose for the longest time not to pay attention to them. When educators said cuts to the school system would hurts kids, he didn't pay attention to them, and when nurses and doctors argued against health care cuts, he paid no attention to them either. *

So how would he feel about going straight to the people for their thoughts on the Quebec situation? Cunningham screwed up her courage and asked:

"Oh yeah, sure," said the Premier, looking

---

* It's no wonder that the Premier has been diagnosed with attention deficit disorder.

through the new issue of *Golf Digest*. "Whatever."

So a massive mailing was undertaken. Every residence in Ontario was sent a pamphlet explaining the Calgary Declaration,* the proposal nailed down in September 1997, by all the premiers, with the exception of Quebec's Lucien Bouchard. Instead of being called "distinct," Quebec would be labelled "like, sort of unique, kind of."

Millions of Ontarians were asked to answer the questions in the pamphlet and mail them back to the Harris Tories, who were clearly unprepared by the overwhelming number of people** who had something they wanted to say.

In case you somehow missed the national unity questionnaire, here are the first two questions from it:

1. **Given that the government of Mike Harris has never wanted to know your opinion on any other issue since it took office, tell us what you make of the fact that we want to hear your thoughts on national unity:**

   a) *The Tories must not give a tinker's damn about this issue.*

   b) *It's got nothing to do with a tax cut, so Mike and his advisers not only don't have a position, they don't care that they don't have a position.*

---

* Also known as The Thesaurus Agreement.

** Six.

c) *Next thing you know, Mike will be taking Sid Ryan golfing with him.*

2. **What is your understanding of The Calgary Declaration, also known as the Calgary Framework?**
   a) *It's what they attached the drywall to at Ralph Klein's house.*
   b) *It's like the stampede, only this time there's more stuff to shovel up once it's over and done with.*
   c) *Not really sure, but I'm confident that I understand it as well as the Premier does.*

Finally, we offer you a rare glimpse into the Premier's thoughts: a scribbled note at the bottom of a golf scoring card. "Should try to get Bouchard out on the course. Wonder what his handicap is?"

■ The 416/905 unity crisis

Just because he's been working tirelessly to make Canada stronger doesn't mean Mike Harris has been letting things slide at home on the living-in-harmony front.

For example, tensions continue to rise between the 416 region of Toronto (the number refers to the city's area code) and the 905-area code region that surrounds the megacity. Relations have been strained by arguments over distribution of tax dollars and who pays for what services. Recently, for example, Toronto Mayor Mel Lastman railed against GO Transit, a service used primarily by commuters in the 905 region but heavily subsidized by Toronto.

This rivalry has intensified since the Tories came into office, largely because they swept the ridings in the suburban 905 belt but didn't score nearly as many votes downtown.

Even though it might be politically expedient to cater to the 905ers over the 416ers, Harris is always looking for ways for the two regions to find common ground. He's even established a six-point plan to ensure that this happens.

MIKE HARRIS' 416–905 PEACE PLAN

1. Get Ernie Eves to phone 905ers at random and tell them a 416er is sleeping with their sister.
2. When a 416er goes to eat in 905 country, make sure he gets seated next to the kitchen.*
3. Have the labour minister teach downtown Toronto squeegee kids to target cars with 905-area dealership stickers.
4. Tell Mississauga Mayor Hazel McCallion that Toronto Mayor Mel Lastman is going around doing a hilarious impression of her.
5. Move the Ontario Science Centre, CN Tower, Casa Loma, and SkyDome to Oakville.
6. Designate Whitby the financial capital of Ontario.

---

* Yeah, right, like a Torontonian would ever go out to the 'burbs for a meal.

MEMO #342406
(Correction to Memo #342398)

To: All Relevant Ministries
From: The Office of the Premier

Re: Provincial Employee Appreciation

I've been doing some more thinking about Oct. 19 being the kickoff for ''Provincial Employee Appreciation Week.''

Seems to me we hardly need an entire week to show an employee how much we value his or her contribution. So what I'm proposing is taking Oct. 21 and making it ''Provincial Employee Appreciation Day.'' Setting aside anything more than a day is going to lead to a loss in productivity, and that's something we simply can not afford.

BIG KaⴅOoNa

9

CRISIS 101:
The Tories and Education

How to street-proof your kids against the PCs

When former education minister John Snobelen was preparing his shake-up to the school system, he used the phrase "invent a crisis" during a presentation that was caught on home video. This was, he pledged, the way to implement change.

If we assess the minister's record on how well he delivered on this approach, he deserves full marks. The province's education system, in the wake of Bill 160, which confines all decision-making regarding schools to a tiny corner of the reigning education minister's brain, is in more than "crisis." It is approaching "cardiac arrest."

So it seemed very unfair, on the eve of the historic province-wide walkout by teachers in the fall of 1997, that Snobelen was yanked out of his portfolio by the Premier. He was judged to have lost the public's confidence to deal with the challenges before him, which made his demotion all the more puzzling, since this made him pretty much indistinguishable from his cabinet colleagues.

As rumours spread that Snobelen's head was on the chopping block, there was speculation the Premier would choose someone equally lampoonable, although an education minister who never finished high school would be hard to beat.

Was there a chance we'd get one-time transport minister Al Palladini, whose first move would be to replace the province's fleet of school buses with Mercury Villagers from Pine-Tree Lincoln-Mercury? Or perhaps David Tsubouchi, the first person in the portfolio to introduce the all-tuna lunch program?

But the job was handed over to Dave Johnson, the "Mr. Fix-it" of the Tory regime who weathered the strike by the Ontario Public Service Employees Union and brought a funereal presence to the dispute with the province's teachers. He had much less of a tendency to put his foot in his mouth. It might have something to do with his height. It was awkward.

Fortunately, even if this new education minister wasn't about to make stupid comments on a daily basis like his predecessor,* there was still the Premier to count on. In the days leading up to the teachers' political action, which closed schools across Ontario for two weeks, Johnson was doing his best to keep a lid on things, to hold down the rhetoric, while the Premier blurted that school board administrators, trustees, teachers and their unions, couldn't be trusted to run the education system.** Better that it should be left to a golf pro and his buddies.

When the Premier hasn't been available to say or do something stupid, the backbenchers have been there to pick up the slack. Notable among these has been Terence Young, the MPP for Halton Centre, who ventured on to the grounds of an Oakville high school one day in September, 1997, to give students pamphlets extolling the virtues of the Harris plan for education. One can only assume that it was a very small flyer.

He'd failed to clear his visit with the local school board, which evidently didn't take to the idea of strangers hanging around the schoolyard without permission, be they drug dealers (who are just

---

* John Snobelen was put in charge of the natural resources ministry, where he's been developing standardized tests for the province's chipmunks. "It's important," the new minister has said, "that our chipmunks be able to do with their nuts what chipmunks in Alberta can do with theirs."

** This is what has come to be known in some circles as "thinking out loud," although in the Premier's case, it's more properly categorized as "not thinking, out loud."

terrible about getting permission) or politicians handing out propaganda. And you're unlikely to find anyone stranger than someone who believes what the Harris government is doing to education will make it better. (If you're a parent, you might want to review with your kids the streetproofing rules on this page.)

Young was instructed by the principal to remove himself from the property. "Can you imagine?" he told the *Hamilton Spectator*. "A member of provincial parliament?"

HOW TO STREETPROOF YOUR KIDS AGAINST THE TORIES

1. If a strange man says he can eliminate the deficit and cut your taxes, without it having any impact on the education system, run as fast as you can.
2. If a strange man says schools will be better once staff are totally demoralized and have less time to deal with more students, tell a grown-up right away.
3. If a strange man says you can make the school system better by taking millions of dollars out of it, take down his licence number and call the police.

■ Dave Johnson's more flighty than you might think

Dave Johnson's skills as the education minister are constantly in demand. For example, the Premier has been so impressed with Johnson's steadfast insistence that massive spending cuts to education will not have any effect on the classroom, * that he's decided to use the former East York mayor's skills in other areas. After all, Johnson has maintained that cuts to boards' administrations, increased efficiencies created through board amalgamations, and a huge reduction in the number of so-called "educrats," will save so much money, that a student in the average classroom will never know the difference, provided he never steps into the hallway, which will be gone.

It's no wonder he's been pegged to take on the new provincial venture, Tory Airways. The Progressive Conservatives have established their own mini-airline for provincial business, and instead of becoming the responsibility of Transport Minister Tony Clement (who's been much too busy coming up with new reasons why a motorist's right to run a red light without having his picture taken supersedes your Aunt Hilda's right not to become a hood ornament on a Jeep Cherokee), the project went to Johnson.

To prove that he could run an airline as well as the education portfolio, Johnson recently took some members of the press for a ride in the provincial corporation's plane.

"It has been our aim," Johnson said, mingling

---

* And with a straight face, too. Although ministerial observers are not sure whether Johnson has anything but a straight face.

with reporters in the passenger section, "to run an efficient flight service that can compete with any similar service anywhere in the world. We've gone to incredible lengths to ensure that our cost-cutting measures have not had any impact whatsoever on the actual aircraft, or its fuselage, or its passengers. That is our solemn pledge; no cuts to the plane!"

And with that the plane took off, soaring into the clouds. Johnson strolled along the aisle, chatting up reporters who were in the seats, scribbling down notes and peering out the window.

"Where are we, exactly?" one reporter asked.

Johnson looked out the window. As he surveyed the countryside, his brow furrowed. "I think that's Windsor, or maybe Thunder Bay. Possibly France."

"Wouldn't the navigator be able to tell us?"

Johnson agreed he probably could, so he ambled up to the cockpit to see what the navigator had to say.

"Hello?" the education minister asked. "Woo-hoo? Is the navigator here?"

The pilot spun around. "We don't have a navigator any more, sir. He was laid off."

"Oh," said Johnson. "Well, maybe you or the co-pilot could tell us where we are, then. Some of the boys in the press gang were wondering."

"Uh, well all the co-pilots were let go, too, but I'll try checking my maps here to see if I can figure out where we might be."

Johnson nodded and went back to the press. "You'll notice," he said, with some pride, "that while the bloated support staff may have been trimmed, our plane still comes with a fully qualified pilot, that the plane still has its wings and tail flaps, and landing gear, and that each and every one of you has a comfortable seat to sit in."

"Uh," several reporters jammed into the back of the plane said, "we've had to stand the whole flight because the plane is so overcrowded. What about that so-called average plane size of 25?"

"Mr. Johnson?" It was pilot on the speaker.

"Yes?"

"These maps of Ontario that I've been supplied, I'm not sure just how up to date they may be. This one here, it's labelled Upper Canada."

Johnson laughed. "Why don't you just get in touch with the Tory Airways tower, then, and have them guide you in." To the reporters, he said: "Everything's going to be just fine."

The pilot again: "Sir, there *is* no tower. The people who staffed the tower were among the aero-crats you campaigned against, and they've all been fired."

"Not to worry!" Johnson said. "I draw your attention now to the sliding window shades which have been retained for passenger convenience. And you'll notice that you each have your own folding tray, and a bag of peanuts."

"I had to share mine," whined one reporter.

"All I got was shells," said another.

About then the pilot came walking down the aisle, a parachute strapped to his back. "They just introduced an early retirement package," he said to Johnson. "I'm bailing out now while I've got the chance. Who needs this kind of aggravation?"

He popped open the door, and with a great rush of wind, was gone.

Johnson wandered up to the empty cockpit, and announced, with considerable satisfaction as he pointed out the front window: "There, you see? I know where we are. That's the CN Tower directly in front of us."

■ The new report card

Every new government that comes along wants to reinvent the report card, so why should the Tories be any different? When John Snobelen came into the education portfolio, he struggled with several ideas of how to improve the existing report card, including going to a Siskel-Ebert system, where a child would know if he'd passed by whether he got a thumbs up or thumbs down. (A somewhat similar system was proposed for evaluating teachers, except instead of giving teachers the thumb, they'd get the finger.)

Then Snobelen experimented with cards that dispensed with the traditional A, B, C grading system, and instead used E for "Excellent," S for

"Satisfactory," NI for "Needs Improvement," and TAAP, which stood for "Thick As A Plank." But parents found these new letters confusing, and students put them through the equivalent of a cable descrambler. If an A was now an E, an S a B, and an NI a B, kids reasoned, and they managed to get three E's and four S's, wouldn't their parents still be obliged to get them a new pony?

So Snobelen finally decided on new report cards that not only were clearer than some of the warm and fuzzy ones that preceded them, but reflected the government's back-to-basics philosophy. A comparison of the old vs. new card appears on the following page.

■ The New Curriculum

One day, there was a cabinet discussion:

Premier: I have to hand it to you Dave, and you deserve some credit too, John . . . John? Could someone get Snobelen to stop showing flash-cards to that squirrel? Anyway, what I wanted to say was, we've hacked away at school staffs, given the remaining teachers more students to work with while cutting their prep time, and put a stranglehold on the support services that used to be available to them. What should we do next?

TWO REPORT CARDS FOR SUSIE MINKLEHOFFER, GRADE 6

OLD STYLE REPORT CARD			NEW, IMPROVED TORY REPORT CARD		
Geography	C	Susie has shown improvement this term but still needs to study her maps harder.	Geography	D	Susie couldn't tell a fjord from Florida if an alligator bit her on the ass.
Art	A	While Susie may not be as strong in some subjects, in art she excels. She could easily have a career as a designer, an animator, or a commercial artist. Given her interest in theatre, set design is also a strong possibility.	Art	N/A	Did somebody say Art? Who needs finger-painting skills to sell mutual funds? Does the world need more "artistes"? Course discontinued so as not to turn out an army of sissies into the workforce.
Math	C	Susie needs to work more with flashcards, but her effort is excellent.	Math	D	Susie can't grasp the "revenue neutral" concept, mistakenly thinking both sides of the equation should balance out.
Music	A	Susie has a natural gift in this area, in both composition and execution.	Music	N/A	Only need for this in the business world is for elevator music. Course cancelled.
Theatre Arts	A	A born performer. Susie's confidence soared during this course.	Theatre Arts	N/A	Did Conrad Black ever say, "Gee, learning to play a flower made me what I am today." Course cancelled.

Johnson: What if we announced that we've decided to rewrite the entire secondary school curriculum, and that it's not a long-term goal, but something we're going to do for next fall, even though we don't have a single textbook or a teacher's guide ready yet. We procrastinate so that nothing's in place until the Friday before Labour Day, 1999, just four days before school starts. Then, when the teachers say they need more time, we can crap all over them because they don't want to give up their long weekend to get up to speed on it.

Premier: *(wiping a tear from his eye)* Dave, sometimes you make me so damn proud.

With so little time to draft a new high school curriculum, the province has turned to U.S. educators, and even some U.S. firms, to pull together courses. After all, this government has shown that if you want something done right, you look south of the border, especially if you're shopping for a political philosophy.

That's why we can expect to see the following courses as part of the Ontario high school program in the near future:

- **Burger King Biology:** Students learn to dissect a Whopper, carefully setting aside the patty, cheese, lettuce, tomato, and bun. Or, if they don't like tomato, they can have it their way and dissect it with double mayo. Coupons for free fries are included with every text, which comes in the form of a laminated drive-through menu board. Possible discussion topic: "If cows didn't want to be used in this manner, shouldn't they have done something to improve their lot in life?"

- **Nike Math:** A typical question out of the teacher's guidebook asks: "If it takes the average overseas Nike employee 14.3 million years to make what Michael Jordan makes for a 30-second commercial, is this, like, a great country or what?"

- **The Literature of Microsoft:** What are the hidden truths in the Windows 98 operating manual? How are allegory and foreshadowing used in the development of the various icons? Teachers will pitch their Shakespeare and Hemingway texts to embrace this collection of stories, especially when they find out who's paying for the school's new computers.

- **Coca-Cola Calculus:** Here's a great exercise for children in almost any grade: If Coke agrees to put one pop machine into the school for no charge, and sells the school a case of 24 cans of Coke for $4.80, and the school sells each can for 75 cents, how large a lawsuit might the Atlanta-based corporation launch if kids show up at school wearing Pepsi T-shirts?

■ How the funding formula works

To ensure that dollars for education are directed to the classroom, Queen's Park is now telling individual school boards how much they may spend on things like salaries, supplies, busing, and trustees. It works a bit like this:

A school board nervous that it won't get enough money for the coming year is told that it will receive $200 million. Yeehaw! The board officials are thrilled. That's the same amount of money they had last year. All those nasty things they said about Mike Harris are taken back. The Premier is a hero! So's Dave Johnson! Education spending is preserved! Maybe this government isn't so awful, after all.

The province says: We're glad you're happy. We'd like to take a moment to point out that there are some guidelines as to how this money may be spent. As you know, to ensure that the money is used wisely, the ministry is not allowing boards to spend their allotment of funds as they see fit. Here's how you must spend your cash:

Pencils, textbooks, notebooks, chalk	$10 million
Salaries and busing	$20 million
School maintenance, heat	$5 million
Aircraft carrier	$165 million

Now, the board sees this and says hang on for a minute here, we don't really need $165 million for an aircraft carrier. We can't *remember* the last time a school board in the centre of Ontario needed an aircraft carrier, although it might be nice to have one sitting on the front lawn of our board offices, jet fighters ready for takeoff, the next time the education minister comes to call. But we really might be better off using that money for building some new schools to replace our mouldy, toxic portables.*

Hey, it's your call, the province says. If you don't want to use the $165 million for your own personal Nimitz to cruise Lake Simcoe, consider your total budget to be $35 million. But don't ever let anyone say we didn't offer.* *

■ The role of the trustee

Some critics have suggested that Bill 160 wipes out a community's say in its local schools, and

---

* The problem of mould in portables came about by accident. The education minister had actually intended for toxic mould to be introduced into school administrative centres as a way or reducing staff, but the stuff spread to outside classrooms instead. Johnson had said, in fact, "We do not believe layoffs in administration will be necessary; we'll be able to reduce most jobs through infection."

** Earlier this year Bruce Willis starred in *Mercury Rising*, a movie about a kid who manages to decipher a secret government agency's top secret code. In the first draft of the script, the child actually cracks the Tories' formula for education funding, but producers said that simply defied belief.

that the trustees they elect to make decisions now have none to make. Nothing could be further from the truth.

While it's true trustees no longer have any say about how to spend a dime of their board's budget, and they no longer have a mill rate to set to raise education taxes, there is, as Johnson himself has said, a major role for trustees to play.

Take school washroom policy, for example. Should toilet paper in a stall be hung so that the paper hangs down next to the wall, or should it hang down away from the wall? This is where trustees under Tory rule can make a contribution, seek a consensus, maybe even bring in consultants. Trustees will have to move on to other issues, of course, when the province refuses to pay for toilet paper any more.

■ Finally

To be fair, the Premier's not always wrong about matters pertaining to education. One comment of his that got a lot of attention was his crack that many teachers have time to hold down more than just the one job.

(One wonders what kind of second job a teacher could hold down that wouldn't take up too much time. Senator comes to mind.)

But the truth is, most teachers hold down way more than just one job. Here are a few of the other occupations they spend time in:

- Social worker
- Sexual abuse watchdog
- Nutritionist
- Peacemaker
- Unofficial peace officer
- Diplomat and disciplinarian
- Computer programmer
- Instiller of values
- After-school coach
- Cleaner
- Lunch-time supervisor
- Field-trip chauffeur
- Booking agent for in-class speakers
- Shapers of destiny
- Defenders of the public education system.

While it may be true that they only get paid for the one job as teacher, the Premier's certainly right that today's educators are given the chance to fulfill all sorts of roles.

10

GAMBLING Our Way to Prosperity

> "Betcha we get re-elected no matter what we do!"

Desperate to find cash any way it can to simultaneously cut the deficit and finance its premature tax cut, the Tory government has embraced fundraising methods it decried while in opposition. For example, Mike Harris pledged not to impose user fees, or close hospitals, or hack away at education to balance the budget. Another cash-grab he protested was the proliferation of casinos and other gambling enterprises.

In fact, he had this to say back in May, 1993, two years before forming the government: "There is no doubt that communities in Ontario will change if a casino comes to town. It brings crime, it brings prostitution, it brings a lot of things that maybe an area didn't have before. This is a high price to pay."

But now that the Tories are in power, they've had something of an epiphany and shown a tremendous moral flexibility* when it comes to making this a better province for you and me.

Which is why the Tories have decided not only to embrace gambling, but to crawl right between the sheets with it.

Organized gambling is a terrific boon to any region's economy. The casino itself needs blackjack dealers, cleaners, waiters and waitresses, women in low-cut gowns who say things like "Oooh, do you think you could win one for lil' ol' me?" and at least one guy named "Lenny"** who can toss you through a plate glass door if he catches you trying to sneak a peak at the dealer's hand.

But there are spinoff industries as well.

Just as a major auto assembly plant means business for local suppliers of car parts, a casino means oodles of work for people in the community who used to waste their time doing things like making steel. And that means a shot in the arm for the local economy.

---

* Read "bankruptcy."

** Sometimes "Mick."

First of all, there is the Companion Industry, which employs, we are told, Escorts.* We were looking through the Yellow Pages one day for "escalator," intending to fit one to our Lincoln Navigator to make it easier to get from the driveway to the driver's seat, and came across the "escort" listings. There were so many, we thought it was the names of closed hospitals, except that you don't come across many medical facilities named Penthouse or La Femme Woo Woo.

Then there are the managers of those working in the companion industry, who are not about to be seen trolling around town in a Corolla or a Hyundai. These are the kind of folks who'll be planning to spend big bucks at the local Cadillac, Lexus, and BMW dealerships.

Now, when you figure that 6 per cent** of gamblers are diagnosed as pathological, meaning they would rather spend their paycheques feeding the slots than their families, you just know there's going to be an upsurge in gambling addiction clinics. This is why you often hear about mayors competing against one another, trying to attract to their own municipality a world-class addiction centre. This is not unlike building a new arena to get the attention of the International Olympic

---

* These are no doubt Ford Escorts, obtained at a discount through Al Palladini's dealership.

** This is a real number that I didn't make up. Also, 439 is a real number.

Committee when you're making a bid to host the Games (although bribes are good, too). Once you have a state-of-the art addiction treatment facility, luring a casino becomes that much easier.

Having a casino in town is also good news if you are a face-rearranger, kneecapper, or finger-breaker.

When you're a frantic gambler looking for more cash in a hurry, you often find that the traditional banks, like the newly merged Royal–Montreal–CIBC–Nova Scotia–Toronto-Dominion Bank are less than receptive to your requests for a loan. That means turning to less formal lending institutions, the kinds whose offices can generally be found under dimly let stairwells and at the back of billiard halls.

Now, these lending firms tend to have a more strict repayment schedule, and charge interest rates that would make most banks blush.* If the borrower fails to adhere to the repayment plan, individuals skilled in the arts of intensive bruising and dismemberment are very much in demand. (Another good argument for casinos is that their establishment prevents people with these skills from being lured away to the U.S.) Furthermore, once these workers have applied their skills, it means more work for the local emergency ward.**

So if you've ever sought work in a crisis centre,

* Credit card departments excluded.

** Take a number.

or wanted to work the phones for a suicide hotline, or help out in a shelter for people fleeing domestic violence, get yourself to the closest city with a big casino. You could be missing out on a terrific opportunity!

Even though not everyone lives close to a major casino, the province believes every Ontarian has the right to be able to fritter away his life savings whenever and wherever he wants. To this end, the province is pledging to put a gambling machine in each and every household.

Just call 1-800-SCREW-ME and a provincial cabinet minister will personally come to your home and put a video lottery terminal in your bedroom. No installation charge! No upfront fees! Merely swipe your debit card through the machine when you want to play, and funds will be deducted out of your bank account instantaneously. That way, when you finally tumble into bed around 4 a.m., wondering how you're going to pay to have your daughter's teeth fixed, you can take comfort in the knowledge that your money will be used to make this province a better place to raise our children.

■ How the schools can help

One of the reasons the Tories are supposedly revamping the high school curriculum is to better prepare kids for the working world. Given that a large number of the province's jobs will now be in the games-of-chance industry, it makes sense to

incorporate into the course of study the skills needed to work in this competitive field.

For example, for schools that still have a theatre arts program left after the boards finish deciphering the funding formula, there will be a special teacher's guide on how to mount a musical version of *Leaving Las Vegas*. Won't you be proud when you see your child on stage vomiting as convincingly as Nicolas Cage? In mathematics, children will be taught how to calculate the odds of anyone ever leaving a casino with his shirt still on. While most after-school athletic programs will have gone by the wayside, the province will struggle to find funds to hold extracurricular bouncing championships. Students will be timed in how far, and how quickly, they can toss a Grade 9er across the gymnasium.

Finally, there are more benefits than just jobs. Gambling towns are good for the environment, because there's no actual manufacturing. That's because billions and billions of dollars are changing hands without anything actually being produced or accomplished.*

■ Other ways to fill provincial coffers

Any government that has the moral rectitude to make its money off gambling, categorized by the very cynical and misguided as a tax on the stupid,

---

* In this sense, it is very much like the legal profession.

should have no problem expanding into other areas of revenue. Don't forget that one of the province's arguments for getting into the casino and slot machine business was to force the bad guys out. If people are going to gamble anyway, the province argues, better that the government have a piece of it.

With that in mind, the Mike Harris government is already exploring the following ideas to bolster its revenues:

- **Licenced carjackers:** Why should common street thugs have a monopoly on hauling you out of your automobile, punching your lights out, and making off with your wheels? Registering carjackers (they would have to pass a Ministry of Transportation test and have an up-to-date driver's licence) would bring some order to what has historically been a random activity. Carjackers would be required to give the province 80 per cent of whatever they make selling the vehicles to offshore hot car rings.

- **The Ministry of Home Invasions:** The tragedy of this kind of fundraising activity, as currently practised, is the uncertainty of hitting a house worth the effort. There's nothing more frustrating than busting down the door and finding out the little old lady who lives there has nothing but 14 parrots and every Harlequin novel ever written. But by providing home invaders detailed information gleaned through recent property reassessments, much of the guesswork can be eliminated. Again, the province's take is 80 per cent.

- **Crack:** What the hell, why not.

■ Location, location, location

Mike Harris and Co. need to come up with innovative locations for their money-making slot machines.

One of the best spots would surely have to be the emergency ward of your local hospital. Suppose, while you're waiting several hours for someone to tend to that annoying chainsaw injury, you could kill a bit of time playing the slots. Line up three stethoscopes and you actually get to see a doctor. Line up three beds and you might even get into a room. But get three bedpans in a row and it's hallway medicine for you, buster.

Let's say you're a separated mother waiting month after month for your support cheques. You can't reach the Family Support Plan by phone, so why not grab the kiddoes and hike on down to their offices? Want them to look up your file and see what's happened to your money? Plunk a loonie into the one-armed bandit and see if you can line up three pictures of the Premier.

You won't get your money, but your screams upon thinking that there's more than one Mike Harris will help make the office staff's day a little more interesting.

■ Your opinion counts

Many Ontario municipalities put an extra question on the ballot in the November, 1997 election, asking voters whether they wanted VLTs and casinos in their neighbourhoods. The vast majority of voters said "No."

But fortunately, the Tory government understands that, very often, "No" really means "No opinion," and has therefore interpreted the referendum results in a somewhat different way. Most bookmakers give the government 3-1 odds that it will forge ahead with its gambling agenda no matter what anyone says. If not before the next election, then certainly after.

11

How the HOMELESS Can Help

Drop dead so
I can get my
big-screen TV

In the Mike Harris revolution, everyone is expected to do his or her part. Welfare recipients are doing their part by taking a 21 per cent cut; their children are doing their part by going hungry; teachers not yet able to bail out of the system through the early retirement plan are doing their part by taking on more students with less preparation time; their students who used to count on getting special help with things like speech problems are doing their part by doing without; post-secondary students are doing their part by paying whopping double-digit increases for many college and university programs; nurses are doing their part by learning how to parallel park stretchers in hospital hallways; patients are doing their part by dying while they wait for heart surgery, thereby saving OHIP thousands; homeowners in Toronto are doing their part by paying huge residential tax hikes so that the Tories can finally give tax breaks to businesses they'd previously tried to screw, but had to back off when Toronto Mayor Mel Lastman threatened to choose a new wardrobe for everyone in cabinet.

So nearly everyone has had a role to play in this revolution. Except, of course, the homeless.*

The street folks are getting a free ride. Take a stroll up Bay or Yonge streets and you'll see. Do they have to worry about tax hikes on their residences? Well, duh. No worries there. Do they have to worry about higher tuition fees, or paying to take their kids to the neighbourhood pool, or whether their $37-a-month nutritional allowance during pregnancy is being cut off?

The answer, of course, is no. The homeless don't have to worry about anything.**

The Harris Tories believe that, even though the homeless have as free and breezy and carefree a life

---

* While it may be true that making previous sacrifices on the government's behalf may be what led some folks to become homeless, now that they're on the street, they can't expect to coast.

** Okay, there's freezing to death. But we're talking financial matters here.

as anyone could want, they should still have a role to play in battling the deficit. In fact, the Tories are convinced that the homeless, in their hearts, want to carry some of the burden toward making Ontario the best galldarned place to live in the whole U.S. of A.

But how, exactly, does one go about getting the homeless to make a contribution, given that, for the moment, they have absolutely nothing to contribute?

The Tories tried a user fee on baseball caps. That way, before a street beggar acquired his change-gathering device, a little something extra went to the province.

But this led to a lot of extra paperwork, and if there's anything this government pretends not to like, it's paperwork.

And then the Tories hit on it. The homeless could make a symbolic, posthumous gesture. They could bequeath something to the citizens of Ontario. And it turned out to be much simpler than anyone thought it would be.

First, some background.

In 1997, it cost taxpayers $319,872 to bury 219 people who were so poor that not only did they not have enough money to put themselves six feet under, they had no family with that kind of cash, either. This works out to an average of $1,460 per indigent. Up until this year, the province paid half that cost, with the municipality where the person died kicking in the other 50 per cent.

The province has decided it will no longer pay its 50 per cent, for an average of $730 for every dead, homeless individual.

That means, every time a homeless person dies on the street, assuming of course that his shopping cart of belongings doesn't contain gold bullion, the province is saving another $730 that it can shovel into the tax cut.

It doesn't take a genius to figure this one out. Every time a street person dies, the economy gets a shot in the arm.

Let's see what $730 can buy, according to some typical ads that run all the time in the daily newspapers:

- For $699.99 (that doesn't count tax, which will put you a bit over the $730, but you can chip in a *little*, right?) you can get a really cool fax machine ("true photo quality printing") that doubles as a scanner and a copier. And it does everything in colour! Terrific for a home office!

- A very handsome reclining chair for your home is only $698.

- For one month, you could lease 4.5 Saturns at $161 each. Great if you're married and have a couple of teenage kids who need wheels.

- For only $599 a month (there's going to be $130 left over!) you can lease a Cadillac DeVille. (At the time of this ad, leasing a DeVille qualified you to receive a Cadillac ClubLink Privilege Card, allowing you to "enjoy the world-class facilities at ClubLink golf courses. Benefits include 18 complimentary rounds of golf at select ClubLink courses, plus the right to bring guests at regular guest rates."* (Hey Mike, are you getting this?)

- A deluxe wrought-iron patio set, with table, six chairs, and an umbrella, can be yours for only $799. Again, you have to chip in a little extra, but still a pretty good deal when you think about it.

- How about a home away from home? One week in Puerto Plata or Punta Cana will set you back $779. Or, how about one week, all-inclusive, in Costa Rica, for just $799?

Well, you start to get the idea. So the next time you're in the market for, say, a couple of VCRs (one for the bedroom and one for the family room at $365 each, and be sure to go for that simple one-step recording option) thank a homeless person for doing his part to make it possible.

You won't be able to thank him or her in person, of course. But you could say a little prayer.

---

* "Mandatory cart fees apply."

MEMO #342561
(Correction to Memo #342406)

To: All Relevant Ministries
From: The Office of the Premier
Re: Provincial Employee Appreciation
Just some last minute tinkering regarding
Oct. 19, previously touted as
''Provincial Employee Appreciation Day.''

I seem to recall that when offices
honour Remembrance Day, they have a
couple minutes of silence. And this is
for thousands of war dead! Can anyone
tell me how provincial employees rate
more than that? So, still on Oct. 19,
we'll be having a ''Provincial Employee
Appreciation Minute.''

Please let me know which employee you
think is worthy. Out of the thousands
we've got, there must be one. Maybe
someone who hands out the pink slips.

Attilla

12

Getting Ready for ELECTION 99

Kinder,
gentler
my ass

As the Harris Tories near the end of their first term in office, the big question is: Will there be a second? Maybe not. That's not to suggest that the Tories will lose the next election; there are hints that there might not be another one. Mike Harris is said to be working on a new bill, the Democratic Enhancement Act, that aims to cut the fat out of democracy by eliminating those aspects of the system that are so costly: namely, the casting and counting of votes. For example, Tory studies have shown that millions of dollars are wasted tallying the votes of people who don't even get elected.

However, this idea's still on the back burner, so in the meantime, the Common Sense Revolutionaries are doing everything they can to prepare for an election, most likely in 1999. Much of that preparation has to do with recrafting the image of their party and, in particular, their leader, who has, they fear, not always have come across as a sweetheart. Go figure.

Harris has been categorized as insensitive, uncaring, oblivious to the suffering his government has inflicted. He's been branded a bully. Mel Lastman has gone so far as to call him a liar (then kissed and made up with him).

How did this come to be? Could it have anything to do with three years of unrelenting cutting and slashing to the provincial workforce? Could there be a connection between his poor numbers with female voters and that reference to Women's College Hospital, the symbol of commitment to women's health care in Ontario, as a "dingy old building?" Could his reputation for lack of compassion be at all linked to his comment that laid-off health care workers are no different than the folks who used to make hula hoops?*

You think?

In fact, the Tories have recognized that they've got something of a crisis on their hands where

---

* Interpretation? Quality health care is a fad, along the lines of goldfish swallowing, flagpole sitting, and Pog collecting.

women are concerned. While Harris continues to win high marks from older, white males, he consistently gets a failing grade from women when the polling numbers come in, mainly because the areas where he's made the deepest cuts, health and education, impact on women more than men.

Aide: Mr. Premier, we need you to score better with women.
Premier: Woo-hoo! When do we begin?

It was the Dionne Quintuplets episode that crystallized things for many people. Not only did this show Mike Harris sticking it to women; he was sticking it to elderly women. A double-play. A two-fer.

When the Premier first learned that Cécile Dionne was looking for a better settlement for herself and her two remaining sisters, he said: "What the hell, didn't she make enough off that song she did for Titanic?"

After aides straightened out the Premier, they were able to get down to the serious issue of what might be a reasonable offer for the surviving Dionne Quintuplets, who, as children, were made wards of the province, which turned them into zoo animals.

These backroom negotiations became public during a meeting of the Tory caucus up in Collingwood, where the major item on the agenda was reshaping the party's image.

As if to underscore this, the Premier stepped

outside to talk to the press for awhile, explaining that the province's current compensation package for the Dionnes* was the absolute final offer. If the sisters weren't happy with it, Queen's Park would be siccing the dogs on them.

This didn't play as well on the six o'clock news as the Premier's handlers had hoped, especially when one station did a re-enactment of the dog threat using oversized Cabbage Patch dolls and a Doberman.

Something, the backroom Whiz Kids decided, had to be done.

■ The Sixth Toe Theory

About halfway through the first term, a photograph surfaced, showing the Premier in 1967, wearing a swimsuit and clutching a bottle of beer. A closer inspection of the photo appeared to reveal a sixth toe on the Premier's right foot. The press went wild. Was the Premier some kind of mutant? Was he the product of a radioactive spill? And should this guy ever go around in a bathing suit again?

Desperate to get to the bottom of the most fascinating development in the history of the Ontario government, reporters persuaded Harris to take off his right shoe and sock for the cameras, so that a

---

* Unlimited lifetime supply of tea and doilies and a free weekend at Casino Rama.

picture guaranteed to ruin the breakfast of thousands of Ontarians could be splashed across the front pages of the province's newspapers. There were five — count 'em — five toes. But not everyone was convinced.

Many* theorized that the sixth toe did exist at one time, but was surgically removed and — here comes the really scary part — preserved.

In much the same way as the evil empire in Woody Allen's *Sleeper* planned to clone a new leader from the leftover nose of the old one, so too did the Tories undertake a secret project to make some backup premiers and keep them in storage until the time was right. The plan became known as "The Kinder, Gentler Project."

There were hopes the clones would never be required. Advisers worked closely with the real Premier in an attempt to soften his image, to make him seem more compassionate, to make him, in the words of one spin doctor, "cuddly."

Just when they'd think they were making progress, the Premier would stand before the cameras and make a comment like the one about the Dionnes. Or, in a bid to belittle participants in an anti-Harris rally, he'd joke about how an Iraqi or Iranian group decided to join the parade, sparking outrage and requiring an apology. Or, in defending the elimination of a $37 nutritional allowance for

---

* See Gunmen, Lone (*The X-Files*).

pregnant welfare moms, he'd say he didn't want them spending it on beer.

Medical specialists conducted several brain scans on the Premier in an attempt to determine whether he was missing that vital part that prevents the mouth from automatically saying things the brain is thinking.*

This is the part that normally keeps a person, upon meeting someone with a bump the size of a rutabaga on his nose, from saying: "Whoa, that bump on your nose is the size of a rutabaga, isn't it?"

This is what doctors found when they developed the x-rays of the Premier's brain:

MR. SILLY GOLF AND COUNTRY CLUB FRONT 9

HOLE	PAR	PLAYER 1	PLAYER 2	PLAYER 3	PLAYER 4
I	3				
2	5				
3	4				
4	4				
5	5				
6	3				
7	5				
8	4				
9	4				
Total	37				

* Missing this part has made Howard Stern a millionaire.

OPPOSITION STRATEGY

What tactics will Dalton McGuinty's Liberals and Howard Hampton's New Democrats employ in the next election?

One might think that with all the opposition to the Harris agenda, these two parties would have their re-election plans all laid out.

The Liberal strategy is simple: Find Dalton. There have been few confirmed Dalton sightings since he became leader in 1996, although there were a few false ones at the annual Norman Bates Lookalike Convention. He has, however, been seen regularly on the sides of milk cartons.

As for Hampton, he's already got two slogans. The first, "Don't know Bob Rae, never have" may distance him from the party's disastrous past. But once the election begins, and it's clearly a show-down between the Liberals and Tories, you're also likely to hear: "Hey, I'm over here!"

"Dear God," said the first x-ray technician to look at the film. "An empty score card."

The Premier's handlers knew the time had come for Plan B. It was time to send in the clones. "We're sending you away," the Whiz Kids told the Premier one day in April, 1998. "A golfing holiday."

"Great," the Premier said. "I could use a break. How long will I be gone?"

"Until after the next election."

Mike Harris shrugged. "Oh, I get it. It's time for one of the Toe Guys. That's cool. But there's two things. One, if his swing stinks, no photo ops on the golf course. I don't want my reputation ruined. And he doesn't go home to Janet. I saw *Face-Off* and it gave me the willies."

Everyone agreed. Harris was enrolled in the Premier Protection Program, shipped off to Florida (plenty of courses in the neighbourhood) and given, temporarily, a new identity as a book shop owner. The Whiz Kids figured if anyone ever got suspicious, they'd never look for him in a job like that.

The very next day, a new "Premier" was on the job. Which explains why someone who looked like Mike Harris and talked like Mike Harris but wasn't Mike Harris was all of a sudden using words like "compassion" and "decency" and announcing that Ontario was putting up more money for the Hepatitis C victims. The clone was there for the reading of the spring, 1998, Throne Speech, which attempted to paint the Tories as caring and receptive to new ideas.

One night, he even filled in on CFRB, conducting a phone-in *Frasier*-style show. "I'm Mike Harris, and I'm listening."

But then one day, taking calls on that same station, he was asked how he felt about a separatist being hired to be a hospital administrator in Ottawa. "Well, seems to me you'd be better off with someone who believes in Canada, even if

143

that someone's a satanic serial killer who eats the still-beating hearts of his victims. But that's just my opinion."

Clearly, the "kinder, gentler" plan was not foolproof. The clones were equally adept at putting not just a toe, but an entire foot, in their mouths. There was something in the genetic makeup that couldn't be altered. There's talk now that the real premier might as well be brought back. It just doesn't make any difference.

■ Getting out the message

The Premier can't be expected to carry the ball all the time in defending the government's actions. His MPPs, including the backbenchers, must be out there, all the time, promoting the government's accomplishments, deflecting criticisms, turning bad press into good press.

One of the most visible Tory pitbulls is Steve Gilchrist, MPP for Scarborough East. He frequently appears on radio and television news programs to debate the issues with fellow panel members Frances Lankin, New Democrat MPP, and Liberal MPP Gerard Kennedy, who was on the way to becoming his party's leader until the membership decided to include in its platform a clause stating that it had no interest in forming the next government.

Moderator: What are we to make of the provincial ombudsman's report that says basic services in this province are crumbling? There are lineups everywhere, waits of up to seven years for some things.

Lankin: It's real evidence that this government has moved too fast, that it has put saving money ahead of helping people.

Kennedy: I agree. This report is an indictment of Tory neglect.

Gilchrist: *Grrr! Rrrr! Rufff! Grrrrrr!*

Lankin: I think even Steve here would concede that when a provincial official condemns the level of service, it's time to take notice.

Gilchrist: *Rrrrrrrrrrr. Rarrr! GRRRR!*

Kennedy: I hate to be a bother, but Steve just bit me. Does anyone know whether he's had his shots?

The Tories, as they attempt to figure out why some segments of the population still revile them, have complained repeatedly that they're having trouble communicating their message.

It's the media's fault, they say. Or it's our political opponents' lies, Mike Harris charges. One thing the political opponents haven't been able to do, however, is spend millions of dollars to send 10-page pamphlets to every last household in the province; pamphlets that say right on the front page "We need your input" and then leave a total of three lines inside for you to write down your suggestions.

Anyway, the Whiz Kids are still at it. They're busy drafting The Common Sense Revolution II, The Sequel, working night and day to find just the right phrase to catch the voter's imagination; something as strong as "Common Sense, For a Change." That was a winner back in 1995.

Without appearing to go soft, how do you tell the public that you know your "tough love" policies were the right thing to do, but that now you're prepared to listen, to move a little more slowly, to pull your punches, to turn over a new leaf? How do you communicate that in only a few words?

After coming up with dozens of phrases and bouncing them off focus groups, Mike Harris thinks he's finally found one that'll make the perfect bumper sticker in the next election. It is:

> ### I PROMISE I'LL NEVER HIT YOU AGAIN

Works for me.

Suggested Readings

To gain an even better insight into how the Tories developed their philosophies and the Common Sense Revolution, you might want to read some of the material they did. This is only a partial list:

- **The Golfer's Book of Wisdom: Common Sense and Uncommon Genius from 101 Golfing Legends**, by Criswell Freeman.

- **A Can of Tuna: The Complete Guide to Cooking with Tuna**, by Andy Black.

- **His Way: The Unauthorized Biography of Frank Sinatra,** by Kitty Kelley.

- **Franklin Is Bossy**, by Paulette Bourgeois and Brenda Clark.

- **Nurse Alice in Love**, by Theresa Charles.

- **Managing for Dummies**, by Bob Nelson and Peter Economy.

- **Politics for Dummies**, by Ann DeLaney.

- **My Teacher Is an Alien**, by Bruce Coville.

- **Curious George Goes to the Hospital**, by H.A. Rey.
- **The Berenstain Bears and the Bully,** by Stan Berenstain and Jan Berenstain.
- **The Right Stuff**, by Tom Wolfe.
- **I Can't Always Hear You**, by Joy Zelonsky, Shirlee Jensen, and Barbara Benja.
- **I've Been Rich. I've Been Poor. Rich is Better**, by Judy Resnick, and Gene Stone.
- **Managing With a Heart: 205 Ways to Make Your Employees Feel Appreciated**, by Sharon Good.
- **Spot Goes to School**, by Eric Hill.
- **My Gun Is Quick**, by Mickey Spillane.

DATE DUE